Business Communications

Don ☰

Related titles in the series

Accounting
Auditing
Book-keeping
Business and the European Community
Business Environment, The
Business French
Business German
Business Italian
Business Law
Business Spanish
Business Studies
Commerce
Cost and Management Accounting
Economics
Elements of Banking
Financial Management
Management Theory and Practice
Marketing
Organizations and Management
Statistics for Business

Business Communications

David Nickson

Suzy Siddons

MADE SIMPLE
B O O K S

Made Simple
An imprint of Butterworth-Heinemann
Linacre House, Jordan Hill, Oxford OX2 8DP
A division of Reed Educational and Professional Publishing Ltd

 A member of the Reed Elsevier plc group

OXFORD   BOSTON   JOHANNESBURG
MELBOURNE   NEW DELHI   SINGAPORE

First published 1996

British Library Cataloguing in Publication Data
Nickson, David
   Business communications
   1   Business communication
   I   Title   II   Siddons, Suzy, 1942–
   658.4'5

ISBN 0 7506 2572 4

Composition by Genesis Typesetting, Rochester, Kent
Printed and bound in Great Britain by Martins the Printers, Berwick-upon-Tweed

Contents

Foreword

To be asked to write a foreword to a guide to good communication, feels very much like being offered a do-it-yourself hangman's kit.

Like most people, I have had to learn to communicate at work by trial and error. The worst of it is, each time, for each purpose, you only get one chance to get it right. What is more, it is hard to be brief and still feel confident that you have said all you need to say. What needs to be said is often not welcomed; and senior people in particular are famously impatient of jargon and detail.

Communication is a mine-field for all of us. Yet success in business is all about effective communication – with our customers, our bosses and each other. In a long career in business management and in boardrooms, speaking regularly at conferences and broadcasting, I continue to get many opportunities to make mistakes in communication by overlooking simple disciplines.

Unfortunately, we each use language in a slightly different way. The English language is particularly open to misinterpretation, because it is so rich in nuance, idiom and jargon. Eliza Dolittle was mistaken for a Hungarian princess because her English was so perfect – she had obviously had to learn it. Once she had cleaned up her accent, she still had to learn to express herself with elegance, while retaining her own essential personality and cockney charm. As Professor Higgins knew, communication is a science as well as an art.

David Nickson and Suzy Siddons have also set themselves a challenge. They will be judged on how effective their own communication skills are, as we read their book. We are in safe hands. David Nickson is an expert communicator, not only with businesses and people, but also with computers, aeroplanes, his guitar and two cats with very short attention spans. Suzy Siddons coached me and my colleagues through our presentations at the London Stock Exchange when, many years ago, we set up our first-ever Senior Management Conference and we have worked together on several projects since then.

This is a serious book. Thankfully, it is also highly practical and demonstrates that other important business tool – the use of humour.

(As my name suggests, I am actually Welsh but I can only manage the National Anthem and a few polite greetings. No one has yet mistaken me for a Hungarian princess, but I live in hope.)

RHIANNON CHAPMAN

(Formerly Personnel Director of the London Stock Exchange and Director of The Industrial Society, Rhiannon Chapman now holds a number of senior appointments in the private and public sector. She also heads her own business advisory service, Plaudit.)

1   Introduction

'Good communication is stimulating as black coffee, and just as hard to sleep after.' Anne Morrow Lindbergh. *1955.*

Business communications covers a wide range of topics, including: presentations, reports, proposals, letters and faxes, electronic mail, interviews and appraisals, negotiations, conflicts, and team working. In fact, communication is key to most of what people have to do in their working life, and much of their non-working life as well. In order to work effectively you have to communicate effectively, and the goal of this book is to help you achieve this.

Business Communications Made Simple has been designed to meet the needs of two groups of readers:

- those who are studying for a business qualification, including GNVQ, A-level, college and first-year university students;
- people in business who wish to improve their communication skills to improve their effectiveness and career prospects.

To deal with these different audiences we have structured this book so that it can either be used as a text book in conjunction with a course of lectures and related tutorials, or to meet the needs of a self-taught student.

To do this the book has been built around a core chapter, Chapter 2 – Effective Communication – which covers the basic theory of communication and should be read before any of those that follow it. In particular it explains where communication goes wrong and why and what you can do to make it right. Chapters 3 to 9 apply this theory to communicating in specific business situations: presentations, reports and proposals, correspondence, e-mail, interviews, appraisals, negotiation, conflict handling.

When you have read Chapter 2, and are familiar with its concepts, the other chapters can be dealt with in any convenient order. This means that it can be used either as a linear study course, or to meet your specific requirements.

In addition, three chapters deal with communication on a broader front. Chapter 10 covers a topic that is not immediately obvious as a component of a book on communications – time management. However, making sure you have the time to communicate efficiently, is a prerequisite for being able to put the lessons of this book into practice and we recommend that you at least glance at this chapter to make sure that poor time management is not prejudicing your ability to communicate. Chapters 11 and 12 expand the scope from point issues to the wider implications of communicating effectively in business: – working in teams, how interactions affect people working together, and the communication skills they need; and teleworking – working from home – special communications issues related with remote working, together with an assessment of the advantages and disadvantages of this way of working.

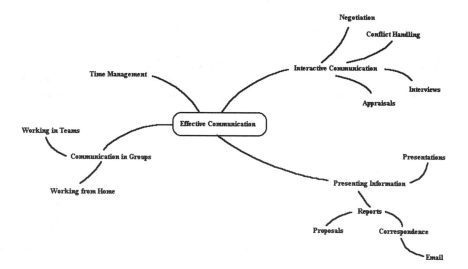

Figure 1.1 Mind-map of Business Communications Made Simple

Figure 1.1 is a mind-map of the book, which shows how the various chapters are linked together, and indicates the flow of thought that was followed in producing this book.

Note that the nature of the subject being covered does not allow everything to be neatly categorized, so there is overlap between the subdivisions. For example, telephone technique is most definitely an interactive communication, but it has been dealt with in the section on 'working from home' because it is very much part of day-to-day office life in the way that dealing with the daily post is. Arguably, it could have been dealt with in one of the 'interactive communication' chapters or even in the 'communicating in groups' section of the book. We are well aware that the placing of some of the information in this book could be open to debate and ask you to be tolerant of what may seem like logical inconsistencies. The important thing is that the information is presented so that it can be readily understood and that has been the overriding principle.

Figure 1.1 shows the core chapter of the book is Effective Communication (Chapter 2) from which four main areas relating to business communication have been derived:

● Presenting Information: giving out information to an audience, either in person or via some form of written/electronic media. This includes presentations, reports and proposals, and correspondence, including the use of electronic mail. (Chapters 3, 4, 5, 6)
● Interactive Communication: studying communication skills that are needed for dealing with people interactively. The situations covered include interviews and appraisals, negotiation and conflict handling. (Chapters 7, 8, 9)
● Time Management: an adjunct to effective communication. Tools are provided to allow you to organize yourself so that you have sufficient time to communicate effectively. (Chapter 10)
● Communicating in Groups: these chapters deal with the communication issues of working in groups, such as team working, and working from a home base. (Chapters 11, 12)

The answers section at the end of the book gives sample answers to some of the questions and includes ideas for the content of some of the discussion points. The main function of this chapter is to allow you to find your way round the book and have a good idea of what information it contains. However, we want to reassure you that they have put as high a value on readability and enjoyment as we have on hard facts, and hope that it is, above all, as much fun as you can decently expect to get out of a business book.

'You cannot speak of ocean to a well-frog – the creature of a narrower sphere. You cannot speak of ice to a summer insect, creature of a season.' Chuang tzu, *'Autumn Floods'*, BC 4th–3rd.

'When the eyes say one thing, and the tongue another, a practised man relies on the language of the first.' Ralph Waldo Emerson, *'Behaviour'* *The Conduct of Life* (1860).

'A good listener is not someone who has nothing to say. A good listener is a good talker with a sore throat.' Katherine Whitehorn, *The Public Speaker's Treasure Chest.*

2.1 Introduction

The Oxford English Dictionary *defines 'communication' as:*

The imparting, conveying or exchange of ideas, knowledge etc., (Whether by speech, writing or signs) Interchange of speech . . .

and to 'communicate' as:

To give to another as a partaker; to impart, confer, transmit, to share with, to use or to enjoy in common with, to participate . . .

Webster's New Collegiate Dictionary *defines 'to communicate' as:*

To transmit information, thought or feeling so that it is satisfactorily received and understood.

The ability to communicate is at the core of all shared endeavours. Poor communication is the cause of practically all breakdowns in business relationships.

Here is an example of what can happen between two intelligent, well-meaning and professional people who *thought* that they were communicating:

David: Have you finished the chapter that I asked for?
Suzy: 'What chapter?'
David: 'The one that's got to be presented on Thursday.'
Suzy: 'You never told me that it should be ready for Thursday.'
David: 'Well it has, so you'd better get on with it.'
Suzy: 'Well I can't, I'm doing this magazine article and I want to finish it by the end of today.'
David: 'But I promised Caroline that she could have it for the marketing meeting.'
Suzy: 'Then you'd better write it yourself.'

Here is another:

Suzy:	'The printer's not working.'
David:	'Go into set-up.'
Suzy:	'Where's that?'
David:	'In the print command.'
Suzy:	'Where's that?'
David:	'At the top of the screen.'
Suzy:	'Which screen?'
David:	'Can't you do anything for yourself?'
Suzy:	'Aaaaaargh!'

Breakdown in communication! What went wrong?

Well, the process of effective communication is often a great deal more complicated that it would seem at first. There are several stages that people go through when they are trying to communicate and lack of care at any of these stages leads to confusion and enormous amounts of wasted time and energy.

2.2
The communication cycle

Let's look at the basic communication cycle. These are the stages that occur:

1 The need or desire to communicate with someone else – thinking, feeling, planning internally, setting objectives (aiming)
2 The translation of internal thoughts and feelings into an external means of transmitting them as a coherent message (encoding)
3 The transmission of the message (spoken, pictorial, written, body language, inflection, tone of voice, timing, visibility) (transmitting)
4 The reception of the message (how and why people listen) (receiving)
5 The translation of the message to internal thoughts and feelings on the part of the receiver (decoding)
6 The need or desire to respond to the message that has been sent (thinking, feeling, planning internally, setting objectives) (responding)

There is one cardinal rule to remember for successful communication: *the meaning of the message is the responsibility of the sender and not the receiver.* This is not to say that the receiver has no responsibility for the interpretation of the message; after all, if we do not listen carefully it is highly likely that misunderstandings will occur, but that the main points that we need to consider when we are communicating are: *'Have I thought about how the receiver is going to understand what I am saying? Is the receiver ready to receive what I am about to say? How can I make my message clear? What do I want the receiver to do with my message?'*

2.2.1
Communication scenarios

Take this scenario: you have just had a great idea that will save your boss at least an hour a day in office work. You are really excited about this and ring her up and tell her all about it. She appears to listen to you but later in the day when you get a chance to talk to her she seems very vague about what it was you told her.

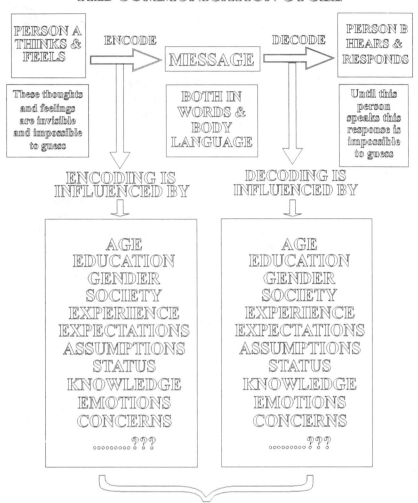

THE COMMUNICATION CYCLE

PERSON A THINKS & FEELS — ENCODE → MESSAGE — DECODE → PERSON B HEARS & RESPONDS

These thoughts and feelings are invisible and impossible to guess

BOTH IN WORDS & BODY LANGUAGE

Until this person speaks this response is impossible to guess

ENCODING IS INFLUENCED BY

DECODING IS INFLUENCED BY

AGE
EDUCATION
GENDER
SOCIETY
EXPERIENCE
EXPECTATIONS
ASSUMPTIONS
STATUS
KNOWLEDGE
EMOTIONS
CONCERNS
???

AGE
EDUCATION
GENDER
SOCIETY
EXPERIENCE
EXPECTATIONS
ASSUMPTIONS
STATUS
KNOWLEDGE
EMOTIONS
CONCERNS
???

THE CLOSER THE MATCH BETWEEN THESE TWO THE BETTER THE COMMUNICATION WILL BE

Figure 2.1 Shows the communication cycle: Aim, encode, transmit, receive, decode, respond

Or this: you work on the help desk of a high-technology company. One evening, just as you are about to leave, the phone rings and a customer asks for your help. He says, 'What can you do about the tractor feed for my PS456 printer?' You reply, at great length, telling her all the options for the tractor feed and offer to send her a leaflet detailing the add-on hardware and software than can make her tractor feed more efficient. There is a long silence, then she says, 'Thank you for the information, but I only wanted to know when it was going to be delivered.'

An understanding of just what happens during communication would have helped both these scenarios, so let's look at the stages in the communication cycle in the order in which they occur.

2.3
Stages in the communication cycle

2.3.1
Aiming

In business, where time is at a premium, we need to think carefully about just what it is that we need to communicate and to whom. A scatter-gun approach is not particularly effective. While there may be times when it is necessary to communicate with every single person in your organization at once, these are few and far between.

Types of information

Here is a list of types of information that are often needed in companies. Which would be the sort of information that every single person in an organization would need to know?

- Complete organization relocation
- Purchase of word processors for sales department
- Large redundancy project
- Change in organization car policy
- New PA for the Managing Director
- Appointment of new directors
- New parking restrictions in the car park
- New tax laws affecting sales
- Significant change in products/services
- Change in health and safety regulations
- Salary rises for the support-desk personnel
- Holiday arrangements for switchboard staff

Having decided what it is that you need to communicate and whom you are going to communicate with, you then need to consider the impact this information will have – will it alarm people, will it make them more efficient, irritable, more comfortable, resentful, safer, happier, bored, more productive, better informed, more motivated or more loyal? The impact that your communication will have on the productivity of your organization should be a primary concern, particularly if you are the bearer of bad news or your message is concerned with a change that will affect the working life of others. Think about the questions people will need answers to, ask yourself what you would feel if you were hearing this for the first time, decide just what you want your audience to do after you have communicated with them, think about the actions and changes that your communication will cause.

Now you need to think how you can make your message of interest or importance to the receivers. Obviously the sender is very likely to be interested in or concerned about what they have to say, but this may not always be true for the receiver. The more you can personalise your communication to fit with the needs and interests of your audience, the better that information will be received and acted upon.

This is why you also need to think of the best vehicle for your message: is it the sort of information that could be posted on a bulletin board, sent in a memo, presented to a group at a formal meeting, talked about face to face, put into a formal report, discussed informally at the coffee machine, broadcast across the e-mail network, put into a letter, legal document, manual, instruction list, put on a poster or video screen, announced over a public address system, teleconferenced or sent out as a press release?

Discussion

What modes of communication exist in your organization? Could these be improved? Which is the most used method of communication in your organization? Is this efficient?

Prioritization

And finally, in this '*aiming*' stage of the communication cycle, how could we prioritize our information and put it in the most succinct way possible? It often helps to list the information you are going to send and then prioritize the points into categories like these:

- Must know
- Important to know
- Helps understanding, gives examples
- Nice to know
- Interesting but not important
- Peripheral to most of the audience
- Padding

This prioritization is particularly important when communicating verbally since verbal communication is linear and moves on the whole time, requiring considerable effort on the part of the listener to take in and remember all that was said. Sadly, verbal information is the hardest to remember and the easiest to misinterpret, so keeping to the subject, making your important points clearly and making sure that the information you give is as useful as possible, will increase your chance of communicating successfully.

Aiming checklist

- What do I want to communicate?
- Why do I want to communicate this?
- Whom am I communicating with?
- What do I want the receiver to do with this information?
- What would make the receiver interested in my communication?
- What is the best way to communicate this?
- Have I prioritized my information?
- How much information should I give verbally or in writing?
- Will I need charts, pictures or diagrams?

2.3.2
Encoding

Having organized our thoughts we then put them into words or images. The words and images that we choose are based on our own internal dictionaries, sets of assumptions, prejudices, experiences, gender, status, education, mood, health and many other factors that are entirely personal to us and to no one else. It is often at the encoding stage that effective communication runs into difficulty – no two people are the same (and I speak as a twin!), so it is little wonder that what is perfectly clear to me may not be so to you.

Discussion

What 'family' sayings or special words do you have that would be incomprehensible to anyone outside the family?

Do you use any specialist language at work that is not generally understood by other groups in the organization?

Language

Specialist language serves a very useful purpose among specialists. It identifies exactly what is under discussion and so saves time and minimizes misunderstanding. This is why doctors, the information technology industry, printers, engineers and so on use 'jargon' to talk about what they do. To the specialists, jargon is completely understandable and serves a useful purpose. Imagine the confusion if a doctor described your symptoms to a surgeon as 'He's got trouble with his back and it needs fixing' instead of 'The third lumbar vertebra has collapsed onto the fourth and the disc between them needs re-siting.' Or a computer repair officer reported in to the manufacturer 'The switchy thing in the box has gone on the blink and we need a new widget', instead of 'The disc controller is faulty and we need to replace the SCSI interface adaptor.'

It is when jargon is used to non-specialists that confusion arises. When communicating with non-specialists it is useful to have a glossary of terms, and when using acronyms (such as VDU, CPU) always spell out what they mean and give an example or use an analogy to illustrate technical points. Jargon is only irritating when it is not understood. This is a point to remember when training others in technical skills – here it is important that the learner uses the correct terms so that help and assistance can be given effectively, so from the very beginning they need to learn exactly what these specialist terms mean.

A word about communicating with people who do not share the same first language as the sender. In multinational organizations this is becoming more and more common with divisional or corporate meetings usually conducted in English. English is normally spoken at a rate of 120 to 130 words per minute. Although people are thinking much faster than this (and usually thinking in their first language), a good communicator will remember that non-English speakers are translating internally as well as reacting to what is being said, and will slow down to about a hundred words a minute.

The encoding process relies heavily on the experiences and education of the 'sender'. Our knowledge and experience-base grow and deepen with time, and it is easy to take our own basic knowledge for granted or as self evident. This is a mistake when you are communicating with people who are unfamiliar with your field of expertise. Always check what the receiver is familiar with, and if in doubt, start with a brief resume to cover the basic information that is needed in order to understand the new information.

Finally, on to assumptions – the unexploded mines that litter the smooth path of communication. It is very dangerous to make assumptions, as they endanger the entire communication process. Quite often assumptions are unspoken and therefore unknown on the part of either the sender or the receiver, which is why they are one of the primary stumbling blocks to successful communication. As listeners we very often make assumptions that we know just what the speaker will say, or what the speaker is thinking before any speech has taken place. As speakers we very often make the

assumption that the listener wants to hear what we are saying and will respond in the same way that we do. Logically, when we think about this we know that it cannot be true, but this doesn't seem to stop us. Really effective communicators either make no assumptions at all (very hard to do) or check their assumptions before they get to the main message they wish to send.

Discussion

How do specialist groups of people ensure that messages are precisely defined so that they can be decoded accurately? What codes do they use?

Encoding checklist

- What language should I use?
- What does the receiver already know about what I am saying?
- Do we have a shared basis of knowledge?
- Do we have a shared basis of experience?
- What am I assuming about the receiver and are these assumptions valid?
- What might the receiver be assuming about me that would hinder effective communication?

**2.3.3
Transmission**

Suppose you wanted to watch or record a programme on the television. Would you be happy if the picture was flickering, the sound was fuzzy, someone was drilling a hole in the road outside the window, there was no chair to sit in, the room was stuffy and you were expecting to be interrupted? Would you feel comfortable if you didn't know when the programme was going to start or finish, or whether the video recorder was working? Would you find it easy to concentrate on the programme if you knew that there was likely to be a power cut or a flood or an earthquake? Would you be able to give the programme your full attention if you knew that there were vital things that you should be doing instead?

What would you do to make it possible to watch or record the programme in comfort? These are exactly the things that you should do to transmit successfully. No matter how carefully you have thought about what you are going to communicate, who is listening to you and what they are likely to feel about what you are saying, if the transmission of the message is not clear then you will be wasting your time. It never hurts to check with your audience if you have any doubts.

*Clarifying your
meaning*

Words alone are not enough to get your meaning across if you are dealing with complicated concepts or spatial information. Simple descriptions can be made livelier and more understandable if you use examples, analogies, similes and illustrations. Many people can only understand new information if they see it expressed graphically. Certainly information that is concerned with numbers, percentages, the way things are arranged or placed, will need a visual aid if it is to be understood clearly. A picture truly can be worth a thousand words.

In the transmission phase of the communication cycle we need to be aware of the sub-verbal or unspoken factors that influence the way people receive. Congruence between what you are saying and the way you are saying it is vital. An anecdote that illustrates this happened in a company we were working for a few years ago. This company used e-mail as one of the main highways for internal communication. However, after a while the system became so overloaded with the amount of internal mail that there was a danger of disk space on the system running out. One manager had the very good idea of asking all the e-mail users to restrict their mail messages to less than one page and asked them to limit the number of copies sent out. The trouble was that he put his ideas into a four-page document and mailed it to everyone.

It is no good asking people to be enthusiastic about a new project if you sound depressed or cynical; it is pointless to tell people of an efficient way of doing things if you use imprecise and muddled language; it is ridiculous to present a glamorous new product if the documentation that supports it is scruffy, badly laid out or boring. Appropriate body language will back up your message – inappropriate body language will certainly sabotage it.

Finally when considering the factors that affect transmission, try to give a quick summary of what you have covered. This will be gratefully received since it allows the receiver mentally to recap in their mind what they have heard or read and so respond more effectively.

Transmission checklist

- Is this the right time to communicate this?
- Can the receiver see/hear/read what I want to communicate?
- Will there be any distractions that will make communication difficult?
- Am I going at the right speed?
- Can I add anything to the words I use that will make my meaning clearer?
- How can I check that I am being received?
- Is what I am saying/writing/showing congruent with the way I'm saying/writing/showing it?
- Is my body language, tone of voice, inflection, eye contact and gesture congruent with what I am saying?
- Do I need to summarize?

2.3.4 Receiving

We think *at least* three times faster than we speak. The implications of this are considerable. Because there is a great deal going on inside our heads when we are listening, it is often all too easy to mishear, ignore or genuinely miss a great deal of information – particularly when it is information that has a great impact on us. Written communication is much easier to concentrate on because we can return again to parts that we need to consider carefully, but spoken communication is linear – it moves on the whole time.

The listening process

Figure 2.2 shows some of the things that are likely to be happening to us when we listen.

Receiving checklist

So what can we do about this perfectly natural behaviour? Here is a list of 'listening habits' that will make communication more effective:

- Try to listen all the way through without judging or reacting
- Always ask for clarification of anything that you don't understand
- Check that any assumptions that you have made are valid
- Only interrupt when you are confused or need clarification
- Show that you are listening – nods, 'um hms', eye contact all encourage the speaker to continue

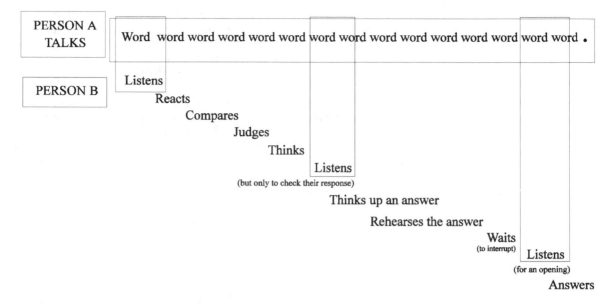

Figure 2.2 The listening process

- Take notes if necessary (but not if it interrupts the flow – we usually write at least three times slower than we speak)
- Look for unspoken messages
- Listen actively, not passively

Communications exercises

Look at the television news. What do the news programme's producers and directors do to make sure that the news is as understandable as possible to as many people as possible?

Listen to one of the science or information programmes on the radio that is repeated during later in the week. How do the producers, directors and performers make the words come alive? At the end of the programme, write a short summary of what the programme was about. Listen to the repeat and see how good your summary was. How well did you listen?

2.3.5
Decoding

If the 'sender' has thought carefully about what he or she is sending, you should be able to decode effectively (in other words – what you have understood should be very close to what the sender meant). If, however, you have difficulty with the message, then now is the time to check out your understanding before you respond.

Ask these kind of questions where necessary:

- What exactly do you mean by ...?
- Could you give me an example of ...?
- Would you repeat ...?
- Could you tell me more about ...?
- So does that mean that ...?

Sometimes there is a natural reluctance on the part of the receiver to admit that they do not understand or cannot follow an argument; this is a great pity since, as we said before: *the meaning of the message is the responsibility of the sender and not the receiver.*

You wouldn't blame yourself if the new car you had just purchased wouldn't start, would you? So don't be wary about asking for clarification.

Decoding checklist

- Don't be afraid to ask for clarification.
- Ask for a glossary of terms where necessary.
- Compare your experiences with what you already know, but don't always trust this if the subject is completely new to you.

2.3.6 Responding

This is where the communication cycle loops round on itself. This time you are the sender and should take all the care that you can, so back to the start of the cycle – *aiming.*

2.4 Summary

The sender is responsible for the meaning of the message.

For successful communication to occur it is not enough to think about what you are going to say and how you are going to say it. It is vital that you consider your audience's needs and attitudes. How you encode your thoughts into words or visuals should take into account the way the receiver will decode that information into their own thoughts. Transmission of all messages should be as painless as possible for the audience, and the sender needs to make sure that what they are communicating and the way they are communicating this information are congruent. Good listening is hard, there is a lot going on inside a listener's head, so good listening habits are well worth trying to achieve. When decoding new information don't be afraid to ask for clarification or extra information. When responding in a communication the shoe is on the other foot and the receiver becomes the sender and is therefore responsible for the meaning of his or her messages.

2.5 Exercises

2.5.1 Relocation

You are relocating your office. This will entail a great deal of change for everyone who works in your group, and some are not happy about the move as it will add an extra half-hour travelling time to their journey to and from work. The relocation will also affect the rest of the organization as they need to know your new address and telephone numbers. Part of the relocation concerns the moving of some highly specialized equipment. New staff will be employed within the next three months.

This is a list of some of the tasks that have to be done:

- Draw up a project plan
- Inform your group of the change
- Inform the rest of the organization of your new location and contact numbers
- Inform your clients of the new location and contact numbers
- Contact the removal company and book the moving date

- Pack up the office contents and furniture
- Unpack the office contents and furniture
- Arrange insurance cover for the specialist equipment
- Involve the technical support department in the relocation of the specialist equipment
- Advertise internally within the company for staff to fill the new positions
- Brief the local recruitment agency on the positions that you will need to fill

(a) For each of the tasks, decide what would be an appropriate method of communication.
(b) What problems could you expect when communicating the logistics of the move to those of your staff who are not happy about the change?
(c) How can you check that all the people who need to know your new location and contact numbers have been informed?
(d) Draw up an agenda for a meeting to inform your group of what changes to expect.

**2.5.2
Good and bad
communicators**

Who do you know personally who you consider to be an excellent communicator? What is it that makes them so good?

Who do you know personally who is a poor communicator? What could they do to improve their communication skills?

3   Presentations

'Folks, You ain't seen nothing yet!' Al Jolson, The Jazz Singer

3.1
Introduction

This chapter covers presentations – a large subject and one which is well suited to taking the concepts of effective communication and making them real. The material provides plenty of opportunity for you to practise what has been preached and will make the ideas presented in the remainder of the book that much easier to understand. Furthermore, mastering the fine art of presenting will stand anyone in good stead in any occupation, with the possible exception of a hermit.

3.2
Definition

pre.sen.ta.tion 1: The act of presenting 2: something presented as a: a symbol or image that represents something b: something offered or given: c: something set forward for the attention of the mind d: a description or persuasive account (as by a salesman of his product) [Webster's New Collegiate Dictionary]

Presentation II The action of offering for acceptance; handing over; delivery; bestowal; gift, offering. III Theatrical, pictorial, or symbolic representation; a display, show, exhibition. A setting forth, a statement. The action of placing, or condition of being placed, in a particular position with respect to something else or to an observer . . .[The Shorter Oxford English Dictionary]

Presentation 1: An ordeal by fire suffered by almost everyone in their business life. 2: A period of extreme boredom where perfectly intelligent people often waste the time of a group of busy professionals who would rather be doing something else. [Nickson and Siddons]

3.3
Why most people are wary about presentations

Giving presentations is a bit like throwing dinner parties; the first fifty or so leave you saying 'never again', and after that it gets to be rather fun. Sir George Jessel said, 'The human brain starts working the moment you are born and never stops until you stand up to speak in public.' Research carried out in the United States some years ago showed that one of adults' commonest fears was public speaking, far outranking fear of flying, heights or snakes! It is natural to be nervous when speaking in front of a group of people, but it is useful to remember that everyone else is just as nervous when they present and will not be nearly as harsh in their judgement of you as they would be about themselves. One of the most effective ways of dealing with presentation nerves is to prepare very thoroughly – and to rehearse at least once for important presentations.

3.4
The presentation process

Let's look at the processes that you need to go through to give an effective presentation. These are:

- Setting your objectives
- Researching your audience
- Choosing the structure of your presentation
- Preparing your scripts
- Preparing any visual aids
- Rehearsing the presentation
- Preparing the presentation area
- Warming up your voice
- Delivering the presentation
- Handling questions
- Following up the presentation

3.4.1
Setting your objectives

A presentation is not a business activity that stands alone. In every case a presentation is a stage in a business process. For instance, a sales presentation should lead to a sale, a product presentation should lead to an understanding of what the product can do, better use of that product or a sale of that product. A management presentation should inform, help a change to happen, ask for more resources or gain commitment to a course of action. A seminar presentation should give people information so that they can perform more effectively or make a better choice, and so on.

Question

Why do people make presentations in your organization? What are they trying to achieve with these presentations? Make a list of the different kinds of presentation you have attended and by each one write what you thought the objective of the presentation was.

You need to set your objectives before you begin to prepare any presentation, and to think about how your objectives fit with your organization's objectives. It is also imperative that you think about what the audience's objectives might be for attending your presentation. If you haven't the faintest idea why they have come to listen to you then you or they shouldn't be there. To set effective objectives you need to do some audience research before you begin to prepare. Here are some of the things that are helpful to find out:

- What do the members of the audience do?
- Which organization do they work for?
- What do they already know about the subject that you are going to talk about?
- What will be new to them?
- How do they feel about you, your group and your organization?
- What is the history of the relationship between yourself and the people in the audience? Do they trust you, will they believe you, what do they know about you?
- What interests your audience, do they have any 'hot buttons' – subjects that they feel passionately about?
- Will anything that you are going to say alarm them?
- What is the benefit to the audience of listening to your presentation?

A benefit is something that will do all or any of the following: make a profit, make life easier, increase the status of a person or organization, make tasks easier, make life more comfortable. save time or effort, increase skills or knowledge base, add value to a product or service.

Armed with this research you can now begin to choose what you will say and show in your presentation, knowing that it will be of interest or benefit to most of your audience. You will also be able to gauge what information would be redundant or of no interest, and you should have an idea of how the audience will feel about you.

These are not the only factors you should consider when thinking about your audience. What about the more intangible factors such as:

- Why do audiences listen?
- Why do they become bored?
- What keeps the audience's attention?
- What will they respond to positively?
- What will they respond to negatively?
- Can a presenter ever expect to keep everyone happy?
- Could a presenter guess how an audience will behave?

These are the eternal questions. Even if you have researched your audience's interests, background, business concerns and objectives, even if you have paid close attention to the way people decode efficiently, even if you have made certain that your communication is clear and 'receiver-orientated', how can you possibly know how they will behave?

Here we move into the murky waters of the personality. Almost any audience is likely to consist of a mix of personality types (the names of these do not matter here, but their characteristics do!). There are 'clusters' of behaviours that you are likely to encounter in an audience so knowing a little about these can help you to tailor your presentation to suit most of the people listening to you.

3.4.2
Pace

'Speeders' (active, adventurous, risk-taking, energetic)

Some people become acutely uncomfortable if the pace of a presentation is too slow, either because you're speaking too slowly or taking too long to make your points. 'Speeders' need to become involved quickly, they need to have their attention engaged with new and exciting facts, new ideas and challenges. To cater for these, the presenter should make sure to start with energy and impact, and to use personal anecdotes that involve the 'speeders' in the audience and address their most immediate concerns. They tend to ask 'when' questions.

'Lingerers' (deliberate, careful, precise, cautious)

These people become uncomfortable if the pace of the presentation is too fast, either because you are speaking too quickly or because the points you are making are coming too thick and fast to give the audience a chance to consider them. 'Lingerers' are happy when they have evidence to consider and options to choose from. To cater for these the presenter should make certain that there is enough evidence to support what they are saying, and should make sure that they have a handout to expand in more detail on what they have said. 'Lingerers' tend to ask 'what' questions. Don't expect a lingerer to speak up too quickly at question time, they tend to be the ones who speak last, and they will appreciate it if you offer to speak to them privately afterwards to clarify their concerns. Don't underestimate lingerers, they are often the advisors to decision makers and treating them as if they are a nuisance will not help your case.

**3.4.3
Priorities**

**'Philosophers'
(thoughtful, strategic,
wide-perspective, far
sighted)**

These people are uncomfortable with 'quick-fix' solutions, they need to know the background to what they are hearing and, even more importantly, to be aware of the possible consequences that might occur if changes are to be made. They respond extremely well to logical and reasoned arguments and pay particular attention to factors such as legality and justice. To cater for the 'philosophers' the presenter should be certain to show that they have considered the long-term effects of what they are proposing, that they present their points logically, and that they consider the impact on the people involved. 'Philosophers' tend to ask 'why?'.

**'Taskmasters'
(efficiency-oriented,
hard-driving, profit
and usefulness
minded)**

These people are uncomfortable with intangible solutions; they need to know 'how much?', 'how long?', 'what proof?', 'what timetable?' – all the facts that will help them to make a cost-efficient and profitable decision. 'Taskmasters' respond well to reference sites, concrete examples and carefully reasoned financial facts. They are extremely persistent and must not be fobbed off with inaccurate answers. Offer to get any extra information they need to them after the presentation, and make sure you do!

**'Humanitarians'
(caring, team-spirited,
group-oriented,
sociable)**

These people are uncomfortable with mechanistic solutions which take no account of how the group will be affected. They like to consider the personal factors in each proposal or change and become irritated if no concern for the welfare of the group is shown. They like to hear what people have said about what is being presented and expect attention to be paid to concerns like personal status and individual motivation; they are not out to harm you, so make an ally of them.

**'Instinctives'
(creative,
individualistic, self
driving)**

These people love new ideas, creative solutions, the chance to develop projects for themselves. They like to use their imagination and creativity and become easily bored if what is being presented is run of the mill or does not allow individual input. They are not particularly obedient and will often try to 're-design' what has been proposed to make things more interesting. To cater for 'instinctives' the presenter should leave an opening for individual input and alternative solutions. They can really lift a presentation with their enthusiastic response.

**'Great experts' (been
there, seen it all,
know better, probably
wearing the T-shirt)**

These people are not here to listen to you at all, they are simply waiting for the chance to show that they are infinitely more informed, powerful, intelligent, blah blah blah! They have a problem, (usually that they don't feel half as important as they want you to think they are), and they're going to take it out on you. Don't take it personally, they do this to everyone, and the rest of the audience is aware of this. To cope, be extraordinarily polite, acknowledge that they have a right to speak and use all the control phrases that you can think of (such as, 'we only have time for one last question', 'does anyone else have an input on this?', and, as a final resort 'eeeaaaarrrrgggghhhh!').

Knowing what to expect from an audience helps you to put in something for everyone and to deliver in a way that will keep everyone happy. Varying your pace, including the information and perspective that each personality requires and being aware that you cannot please all of the people all of the time helps you to keep focused on the audience's needs.

Discussion

What are the things that drive you mad in a presentation? What are the things that interest you in a presentation? If you already give presentations, what are the things that you sometimes do that may alienate any of the personalities talked about above?

**3.5
The presentation
structure**

A presentation sounds best when you deliver it like a conversation; however, delivery and structure are two different concepts. Most conversations are rambling, with interruptions, digressions and meanderings that wind round and round the subject, and may never reach any conclusion. A presentation should be a much more disciplined matter – for one thing, there shouldn't be many interruptions, and, unless you are prepared to commit the cardinal sin of wasting the audience's time, should stick closely to the subject, only including information that adds value to your central theme. This does not mean that a presentation should be dry and boring, but it does mean that every word matters.

As we said in Chapter 2, verbal communication is linear and it is impossible for anyone to recall every word. The audience should go away with a clear understanding of what has been said, and a clear direction to follow and not be overburdened with minute details that overwhelm the main message. This is why you need to prioritize your information.

The human brain is an extremely complicated organ capable of the most amazing feats, however any information that enters the brain passes through a very narrow gateway, and if we try to input more than seven pieces of information at once then 'cognitive overload' occurs, effectively shutting down the brain.

To see cognitive overload in action, get together with a friend and call out four random numbers, which your friend then repeats back. Then try the same thing with six numbers, then with eight. At this point something very curious occurs. Look at the expression on your friend's face – that is what cognitive overload looks like.

The impact of this on presentations is significant, since the brain needs to take information in small chunks it is pointless to try and present everything you know about a subject all at once. This is one of the reasons why we need to structure our presentations carefully.

Basic presentation
structure

Obviously you need to have a start, a middle and end, but what should we put into these stages?

The start

- Tell them what the presentation is about (it helps to have a title slide at this point).
- Tell them what your objectives are.
- Tell them who you are (if they don't already know, your name, job title and contact information should be on the title slide: this gives you credibility to speak on the subject).
- Tell them why *you* are giving this presentation (they may not be aware that you are an expert on this subject or have been involved with the issues under discussion – more credibility).
- Tell them what the background to the presentation is.
- Tell them what your conclusion will be.
- Show that you understand their concerns.
- Tell them what's in it for them (benefits).

- Set the scene for the presentation (the agenda should be on a slide or a handout).
- Grab their attention.
- Set their expectations (when you'll finish, whether there will be question time, whether there will be handouts, coffee, etc).
- Encourage them to listen actively.

The start of a presentation is arguably the most important part of the whole procedure. A bad start influences the audience's view of the presenter's credibility, and it is very hard to recover lost ground. If this sounds as if it all takes a very long time, this is not so. It need only take a few minutes.

Example

'Good morning, ladies and gentlemen, and welcome to Gluewell Industries' Research Centre. For the next thirty minutes (*expectations*) I shall be covering the results of our research into the adhesive qualities of our new super-glue (*what the presentation is about*). At the end of my presentation you will have enough information to assess the viability of changing to this new adhesive for use in the lamination process used in the production of your organization's products (*objective, benefits, understanding audience concerns*). For those of you who do not know me, I am Dr Felicity Ultrastickability and I am based in this centre as the Senior Research Scientist of the Lamination Glues Project (*contact information, credibility*).

'For the last five years, the lamination process has been made difficult by the granularity or "lumpiness" of the glues used. This caused air to be caught between the glue and the laminated layers, leading to loss of adhesive qualities and instability in the finished laminated sheets (*background to the presentation, audience concerns*). I am glad to say that the new glue that we have developed gives none of these problems (*conclusion*). We are also aware that one of your major concerns is the toxic fumes that are given off by many lamination glues. Well, we have some good news for you that will be covered in this presentation (*active listening*).

'I will also be covering the following points: the differences between the old glues and our new products, test results on the stability and effectiveness of the new glues, the conditions under which these glues can be used and stored, and the financial benefits of these new glues. We will have a question and answer session at the end of the presentation which should last about 15 minutes so we will all have coffee at 11.30. If you wish to make notes please do so, but we have a very comprehensive handout for you at the end of the presentations (*expectations, agenda*). (*Pause.*)

'To start the presentation I have a startling piece of information for you. One microgram of our new super-glue is all that is needed to hold the weight of seventeen adult African elephants (*attention grabber*) . . .'

That took about 330 words – a speaking time of less than three minutes.

Exercise 1

You have been asked to prepare a 20-minute presentation to an audience of six people. They are the Financial Director, Marketing Manager, Sales Director, Manufacturing Manager, Logistics Director and your boss. The financial and logistics directors have not met you before. You are a salesperson covering the SE area and are going to give your report on the last (highly successful) six months. You have gained three new clients, expect to do equally well in the next six months and have a desperate need for secretarial help and the help of the Marketing Department in the near future.

You are the best salesperson in the company. You know that marketing is about to launch a new product and you have made plans for this.

Prepare the opening of your presentation.

Exercise 2

It is open day at the 'Find-a-Job' organization. You have been asked to tell four people that you have never met all about what it is that Find-a-Job does. All you know about them is that one is interested in the services your organization offers, one is a potential supplier and the other two are local government officers who may give a grant to your organization in the coming year. Find-a-Job has a good reputation which is becoming well known. Find-a-Job is a small company with only three departments – recruitment, sales, and support. You actually found your current position through 'Find-a-Job' since you interviewed extremely successfully and they offered you the post of senior recruiter. You want to show the potential customer how good Find-a-Job is, show the potential supplier how rigorous but fair your organization is and get an enormous grant from the local government officers. You also noticed that one of the local government officers was very interested in all the company literature in the foyer and that he seemed very quiet. All four visitors are glad to be out of their offices and have no time constraints.

Prepare the opening of your presentation.

The middle

- Tell them about your subject in detail.
- Tell them logically.
- Tell them in a language they understand.
- Tell them vividly.
- Use anecdotes and real examples to highlight your points.
- Tell them how this information applies to their organization and to them personally.
- Link everything you say to reality.

The middle part of a presentation should back up all the claims you made at the start and should clarify your message and develop your arguments. Don't try to say too much and don't (unless you have been asked to, and know that most people in your audience are interested in this) go into great detail; you can always use a handout for the details and specifications.

You should try to link each of the points you are making so that your presentation moves smoothly from one point to the next. If you feel that you are likely to give too much information, ask yourself the question 'So what? What's the purpose of this?' or see if you can finish the phrase 'So that means . . .' after each point.

If you feel that some of the points you are making are difficult to understand in words alone, use visual aids to clarify them; this also breaks up the evenness of a presentation and allows the audience to concentrate on something other than the speaker.

The end

- Summarize: briefly tell them what the most important points of your presentation were.
- Tell them the benefits that your solution, product, options, conclusions will bring to them.
- Tell them what you want them to do next (the call to action).
- Ask for questions.
- Answer questions where appropriate.
- If the answers take a long time, reiterate the call to action.

● Tell them how to get in touch with you if they need to.
● End with a bang and not a whimper.

As you come to the end of your presentation, a great feeling of relief often sweeps over you and there is a tendency to rush the last words and then stop too suddenly, leaving the audience slightly surprised that you have ended. Really good presenters prepare the end of their presentations so that they finish on a 'high'. You might finish with an anecdote or ask for a decision, or present a final benefit.

Discussion

Listen to three different programmes on the radio or television – a documentary, a chat show and a panel show. How do they finish? What did the presenter do or say that rounded off the programme? Could you use the same sort of thing in a presentation?

3.6 Preparing your script

Reading from a script will give a stilted feeling to a presentation and does not give the speaker as much credibility as apparently speaking off the cuff. However, even the most experienced speakers need some sort of *aide memoire* to make sure that they keep on track and get their facts absolutely correct. When preparing the contents of a presentation it is useful to make a mind-map of what you are going to say and when you are going to say it. Figure 3.1 (opposite) gives an example.

Once you know the points that you will cover, and the order in which you are going to cover them you can prepare a series of prompt cards. We use small index cards with a hole drilled into the left hand corner, all held together with a treasury tag, and we lay out the cards like this example:

CARD NUMBER 6
SLIDE/VISUAL NUMBER 4
Whizzo Washing Powder Features – Main Subject: Product introduction (+ white and red fabric samples)

* FIRST POINT: Uses only 2 grammes per wash
FACTS:Other products use at least 4 grammes to get the same result
EXAMPLE: Weekly home wash now uses half as much powder
BENEFIT TO AUDIENCE: Significant savings
* SECOND POINT: Allows colours to be washed with whites
FACTS: Tests show zero bleeding of colours into whites and no fading of colours (Show samples of fabrics)
EXAMPLE: White synthetic underwear washed with non-colour-fast red shirt
BENEFIT: No more pink vests for your family, time saved in sorting whites and colours

LINK TO THE NEXT TOPIC: These are the benefits of Whizzo, now lets look at the way the product is used.

The best practice when preparing a script is to keep the information as clear as possible, marking down the bullet points and any information that must be absolutely accurate. Always show which visual should be used and where to use it. Keep all scripts as simple as possible.

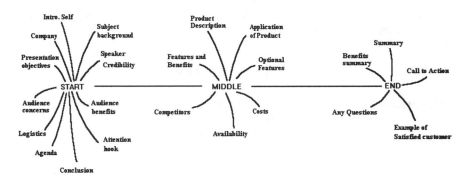

Figure 3.1 Mind-map for presenting a new product

3.7
Visual aids

A good visual aid will do at least one of these things:

- Help the audience to visualize abstract concepts (charts/diagrams).
- Cause the audience to remember what you have said (eye-catching images, humour, colour).
- Show reality (photographs, plans, maps, people's faces).
- Reinforce important and exact information (numbers, exact quotes, financials).
- Link several complex ideas (themes, build-up diagrams, headings).
- Compare information (charts, competitive information, graphs, block diagrams).
- Summarize (short slogans, themes, call to action).
- Introduce (name and title slides).
- Illustrate (artwork, photographs, mock-ups).
- Define (glossaries, codes, close-ups).
- Inspire (slogans, logos, calls to action).

And if it doesn't, don't use it.

A *bad* visual aid will do at least one of these things:

- Make abstract concepts even more abstract (lots of words and symbols).
- Cause the audience to forget what you have said (no colour, no images, poor layout).
- Distort reality (poor graphics, unclear vocabulary, unclear syntax).
- Misrepresent important and exact information (mistakes, inaccurate and misleading numbers).
- Confuse complex ideas (no theme, over-complex diagrams, no headings).
- Define badly (jargon, unknown codes).
- Bore (pompous language, marketing-speak, cliches).
- Strain the eyes (type too small, overcrowding, horrible colours).
- Irritate (messiness, poor placing on screen, lack of focus).
- Give the audience headaches (non-readability, small type, too much on screen).
- Stop the audience from listening (too much complexity, no explanation of what it is about).

If it does *any of these*, don't use it.

<table>
<tr><td>3.7.1
Visual aids summary</td><td>Here is a summary of some of the visual aids available and when to use them.</td></tr>
</table>

THE FLIP CHART

Advantages

Easily available
Cheap
Can be used in daylight/bright light
Informal
No electrical power needed
Can be created ahead of time or as needed
Can be used to record information spontaneously
Sheets can be displayed round room
No particular expertise needed

Suitable for

Small groups
Discussion groups
Informal presentations
Collecting information 'ad hoc'
Training sessions
Brainstorming sessions
Working meetings

Equipment needed

Flip-chart stand
Flip-chart pads (minimum two)
Felt pens (thick, striking colours)
Blu-tac or masking tape

DESK-TOP PRESENTER

Advantages

Looks professional
Easily portable
Interactive
Good in question and answer sessions
Can go to deeper levels if necessary
Relatively inexpensive
Easily updated
Easy to use

Suitable for

Small sales presentations
Business calls
Small group updates
General information
Product listing

Equipment needed

Desk-top presenter
Artwork
Table

THE FLIP CHART

Disadvantages

Cumbersome to carry
Easily damaged
Good handwriting needed
Not good for large groups
Takes up platform space
Slow if created during presentations

Not suitable for

Large groups (over 15 people)
Formal presentations
Prestige presentations
People with poor handwriting
Crowded platforms/speaking areas
Slow writers
Worn out pens, pale colours

DESK-TOP PRESENTER

Disadvantages

Tends to make people think of Jehovah's Witnesses
Not good for medium to large groups
Presentation may become 'mechanical'

Not suitable for

Large groups
Glitzy presentations

OVERHEAD PROJECTOR/SLIDES

Advantages
Can be organized ahead of time
Equipment usually available
Looks professional
Fairly cheap
Frames can be used for notes
Several computer programmes available
Easy to find and show during question time
Quick to make with a photocopier
Room does not need to be too dark
Can be changed/added to during presentations

Suitable for
Small to medium audiences
Most presentations

Equipment needed
Electric power
Overhead projector
Screen
Transparency foils and transparency pens
or computer with graphics program and interface
Printer or photocopier
Frames or sleeves
Table for slides
Ring binder to hold slides

35-MM SLIDES

Advantages
Professional looking
Readable by large groups
Easy to carry slides around
Can use varied imagery
Can be built up for progressive disclosure
Multi-carousel can give simple animation
Computer programmes available for creating them
Vivid colours

Suitable for
Conferences
Large audiences
Formal presentations
'Company' presentations
Standardized presentations
Photographic imagery
Glitzy presentations

Equipment needed
Electric power
Projector
Screen
Slide changer
Dimmable light source
Slides
Carousel

OVERHEAD PROJECTOR/SLIDES

Disadvantages
They need electrical power
Bulbs burn out
Cables trip you up
Screen needs careful siting
Can be clumsy to change
Projector can be noisy
The projector can obscure the view of the platform
Space needed for slides

Not suitable for
Very small audiences (one or two)
Very large audiences (40 upwards)

35-MM SLIDES

Disadvantages
Relatively expensive
Complicated kit
Take time to prepare
Need professional printing
Do not allow interaction
Cannot be updated quickly
Hard to use during question time
Room has to be dim
Kit can be noisy
Need electric power
Take time to stack
Must be stacked and stored carefully

Not suitable for
Small presentations
Informal presentations
Interactive presentations
Question time
Amateur artists/creators

VIDEO FILMS

Advantages
Very professional looking
If created in-house, involves staff
Can be distributed easily

Suitable for
Long-term messages
Glitzy product launches
In-house, in-store long-term information
Distributing long-term messages
Large audiences

Equipment needed
Electric power
Video player
Monitor
Video tape
Sound reproduction
Dimmable light source

For production:
Fully equipped recording studio
Camera
Lights
Sound
Director
Script
A lot of money
A lot of time
Enormous patience

COMPUTER SLIDE SHOW

Advantages
Becoming easily available
Looks very professional
Easily generated (by an expert)
Relatively quick to generate
Allows common design within a slide show
Slide changes easy and attractive
Vivid colours
Easy to operate for presenter
Easily changed/updated
High-tech
Easily distributed
Good at question time

Suitable for
Small presentations
Group presentations (with projector hook-up)
Rolling demos
Point of sale
'Company' presentations
Standardized presentations

VIDEO FILMS

Disadvantages
Very expensive (and perceived to be!)
Not updatable
Room must be dark
Need expert production
Complicated kit needed
Send people to sleep

Not suitable for
After-lunch sessions
Companies doing cost-cutting exercises
Short-term information
Interactive sessions

COMPUTER SLIDE SHOW

Disadvantages
Expertise needed to create them
Possibility of 'computer crash'
Careful planning needed
Hook-up with projector can be complicated

Not suitable for
Large audiences (without projector hook-up)
Amateur operators

COMPUTER SLIDE SHOW (continued)

Equipment needed

Electric power
Computer
Program

MULTI MEDIA

Advantages

Perceived as expert
Very professional
Memorable
Can go to any depth
Allows audience choice
Can be projected to large screen
High-tech
Offer opportunities to 'tailor' the presentation
Can be distributed easily

Suitable for

Almost any size audience (with suitable kit)
Individual viewing
Interactive learning
Training/individual learning
Information exchange
Point of sale

Equipment needed

Electric power
Computer, programme, multi-media hardware
Expertise
Barco or RGB projector for large audiences

MULTI-MEDIA

Disadvantages

Need expertise to prepare
Expensive in time terms
Need complicated equipment
Expensive equipment
Need careful scripting
Takes time to update

Not suitable for

Financially disadvantaged companies
'Quick-fix' presentations
Simple messages

3.8 Choosing your media

Presentation type	Content	Recommended media
Small group, informal, interactive, team meeting	Information update, brainstorming, planning	Flip charts, possibly overhead
Small to medium group, informal, interactive	Information update, company information, long-term information	Overhead, flip charts
Small to medium group, formal, Q/A session	Information, progress reporting, policy information, statistics	Overhead, flip charts
Small group, sales call, interactive	Information, company presentation, product presentation, price presentation	Desk presenter, flip chart

Presentation type	Content	Recommended media
Small to medium group, team briefing, project meeting	Information, planning, discussion, update	Overhead, flip charts, handouts
Small to medium group, training	Information, group discussion, interactive sessions	Overheads, flip charts, handouts, multi-media, video
Medium to large group, seminar, lecture, non-interactive training	General or specific information, not much audience participation, information important to remember	Overheads, 35mm, video, computer slide show

3.9
Rehearsal

The rehearsal allows you to test out your presentation in front of a non-threatening audience, and is essential to a successful presentation. Pick your rehearsal audience carefully. They need to know about your subject matter, the audience you will be presenting to, and yourself. You will probably have to brief them first.

Prepare for the rehearsal, tell your rehearsal audience what you want to have feedback about, show them the visual aids that you have prepared and make sure that you put aside enough time. You also need to think about the questions that the real audience might ask and prepare your answers to these. Critique yourself, as well as asking for feedback from your rehearsal audience. Rehearsals are important for two reasons:

1 They help you to overcome nerves
2 Until you have actually said the words that so far have only existed in your head, you cannot be absolutely sure what will come out when you start to speak.

3.10
Preparing the presentation area

You, the presenter, are in charge of the presentation area. If it doesn't suit you then you should change it round until it does. You will need to check for these things:

● Is there enough space to move around freely? (make space)
● Are there any cables or leads that might trip you up? (stick them down with tape)
● Is the visual equipment in focus and working? (check it out)
● Is the audio equipment working? (check it out)
● Is there anything in the presentation area that obscures the screen? (move it)
● Is there anywhere where you might obscure the screen? (don't stand there)
● Is there anything is the presentation area that might interrupt or dilute your message? (take it down)
● Have you got all the tools, slides etc. that you need and somewhere to put them? (make sure you have)

- Where is the best place to stand? (stand there most often)
- Where is the best place to come on from and to leave from? (make sure you use them)

3.11 Warming up your voice

A ballet dancer wouldn't start a performance without limbering up, nor would an athlete, a musician or a racing driver. Presenters need to warm their voices up too. Here are a few exercises that will help you to so this.
The secret of a good presentation voice is the following:

- Audibility – everyone must be able to hear you.
- Power – you should sound as strong at the end of the presentation as you do at the start.
- Clarity – you need to speak clearly and crisply.
- Modulation – your voice should sound interesting and interested.

Audibility and power exercise

Your voice is powered by your breathing. When we are nervous we tend to gasp in too much breath and hold it in the top of our chest. This tends to raise the pitch of the voice and make us sound breathless. The secret is to breathe out all the old air before you breathe in the new. Take a deep breath, trying to draw the air deep into your chest, and then exhale steadily until you have no breath left. Do this three or four times. This gets rid of all the old stale air in your chest and will make your voice sound stronger.

Now breathe deeply again and count out aloud (slowly) from one to ten. When you get to ten, breathe out the rest of the air and breathe deeply again. This time try to count from one to fifteen. If you can do as much as this, this would be enough. Breathe out again, then in and try from one to twenty. This tones up your diaphragm and loosens tension.

Clarity and modulation exercise

The sounds that make our voices clear are called the 'plosives'. These are the sounds that explode out of the speaker's mouth and out across the audience. The plosives are P, B, T, D, K and G (guh). When you are speaking to an audience, try to make the plosives as clear as possible, particularly at the ends of words. This will give your speech a crispness that is particularly effective for public speaking.
Warm up your lips and tongue with these phrases (said aloud):

- Peter the private detective has perfect pitch.
- Bumble bees buzz busily on berry bushes. Big, bad, bumble bees and big beautiful butterflies.
- Tiny tots and tiny teenagers get tricky trips to Tottenham.
- Dear Dominic does not like drinking draughts of dandelion and burdock.
- King Kong calls for cups of tea at twenty past two.
- Giggling girls gather glorious gladioli in gorgeous gardens.

As you say the phrases crisply, exaggerate the modulation of the voice, sometimes sounding surprised, sometimes depressed, sometimes excited and sometimes bored.
Warming up your voice (usefully done on the way to make your presentation) ensures that the first words spoken to an audience do not come out in a high pitched squeak or a husky whisper.

3.12
Delivering the
presentation

Making a splendid first impression

When they started televising parliament, the MP who made the first speech complained that when you could be seen rather than just heard, only 7 per cent of a presentation's impact was dependent on the words spoken; almost everything rested on image, body language, style of dress, tone of voice and initial impact. Sadly this is true and should be borne in mind when you are making a presentation. You should wear what is appropriate to the audience – a business suit is what normally applies (for men and women). Research has shown that people make up their minds what they think about you within the first 40 (or so) seconds, so if you inadvertently give the wrong impression at first you will have to work really hard to overcome this. It is much easier to give the best impression right up front – and what follows will explain the way to do it.

3.12.1
Stance

This has nothing to do with height, and everything to do with the way you hold yourself. When we are nervous we tend to 'guard' ourselves, keeping our upper arms tight against our chest, or hunching our shoulders; this is a perfectly natural thing to do, but it makes us look apologetic. So, straighten your back, look the world in the eye, and think *tall*.

3.12.2
Expression

Start with a smile, but remember that too much smiling makes people think we are trying to please them too much. When people are communicating with you, listen carefully – there is no need to smile all the time, a nod or a thoughtful expression will pay far greater dividends than an ever-ready smile. Look also at the way people use their eyebrows; high-credibility people seem to have very slightly lifted eyebrows and look alert and interested.

3.12.3
Eye contact

This is one of the most significant indicators of status and competence. It is noticeable that high-status, high-credibility people have greater eye contact than others. They are not afraid to look people straight in the eye, they don't keep their eyes cast down, or look at the ceiling or floor when they are talking to others. Try to keep your eye contact up – people will trust you more, believe you more and know that you are interested in them (there is a significant difference between high eye contact and staring – we all know instinctively what this is and will look away if we feel we are making people uncomfortable). Take care with eye contact when doing business with different cultures; low eye contact to a Middle Easterner will make them mistrust you, whereas high eye contact with the Japanese is considered bad manners.

3.12.4
Speed

Powerful people rarely move fast, so if you want to be taken seriously, don't hurry. A scampering, hasty, flustered person doesn't look as if he or she is in charge or capable of handling a crisis/task/everyday job. Slow down – powerful people take their time (policemen are trained never to run unless there is a real emergency). If you move too fast you'll look as if you're hurrying to catch up, rather than as though you are doing the job competently. If you slow yourself down, you will also give yourself time to think, always useful when time is short and decisions have to be made carefully.

Since it is advantageous to give the impression of being in control, speed is most important right from the first meeting or, in the case of a presentation, from the moment the audience first sets eyes on you.

3.12.5
Space

Throughout history space has been one of the most powerful ways of indicating power. Space is used to show what is powerful, who is powerful and who makes decisions. The more powerful you become, the more space you will be given – a bigger office, bigger desk, car parking space, bigger house and so on. People will even stand further away from you to show their deference. It is said that when Kennedy became president of the United States he found that there suddenly seemed to be an invisible line on the carpet of his White House office which visitors were reluctant to cross.

The way you handle your personal space tells people a great deal about how you feel about yourself. Feelings of self consciousness, shyness, uncertainty, dislike, fear and pain are shown by a withdrawn, minimized body posture and small, inward-moving gestures – usually with the palms of the hands hidden. Self confidence, liking, well-being and happiness are all characterized by an outgoing body image with expansive, outward-moving, open-handed gestures.

3.12.6
Gestures

The best way to make a good presentation is to be yourself; if you are not a person who makes a lot of gestures then it is unwise suddenly to start making them in a presentation; if you find yourself standing stiffly, hiding your hands, and ducking your head this may lead the audience to think that you are not sure about what you are saying. Relax your shoulders first, clasp your hand lightly at waist height holding a pencil or pen loosely, and your posture will immediately improve. Any gestures you then make will be more effective since the pencil or pen will maximize them. Most people are nervous at the start of a presentation, but it is almost guaranteed that after you have been speaking for a few minutes, you will loosen up and look more natural.

Presenter mannerisms that irritate most people in an audience include:

- Lack of eye contact
- Turning your back on the audience
- Pointing or stabbing a pointer at an audience
- Hiding behind the flip chart or screen
- Fidgeting with a presentation pointer
- Not being able to find the right slides
- Standing perfectly still
- Looking only at a script or prompt cards and not at the audience

3.13 **Handling questions**	This is a crucial session in any presentation. No matter how good the presentation has been, if you handle questions badly you will undo all the good that you have done. Handling questions takes considerable discipline. Here is a technique that allows you to stay in control and handle questions effectively. We call it the STOP technique. First, you need to listen to the question all the way through and then, before you answer,

S   Share the question (where appropriate) with the rest of the audience who won't have heard it because they were all too busy thinking about the questions they wanted to ask
T   Think about how you are going to answer the question
O   Only answer the question – don't get side-tracked and don't go into too much detail
P   Politely check that your answer was okay

You should be just as much in control during the question and answer session as you were during the presentation.

3.14 **Summary** 	A business presentation is a step on the ladder of a business process and should be planned with a clear set of objectives in mind. These objectives are just as much concerned with the audience's needs and expectations as they are with the presenter's intentions. A good presentation takes into account the varying personalities, interests, knowledge and experience in the audience and should be constructed to fit with these rather than just the presenter's message.

Careful preparation is essential, using a structure that allows your message to be clearly expressed and remembered, so you need to prepare a compelling start, a clear exposition of facts and benefits in the middle with a memorable summary and call to action at the end.

No matter how well you have prepared the presentation, you still need to consider the delivery – of course you must be seen and heard, but you should also take into account how you will illustrate your points, using visual aids to add value to your message.

Here is a checklist to help you to prepare an effective business presentation.

1   **Set your business objectives for the presentation**
Is it selling? Persuading? Instructing? Scene setting? Introducing? Controlling damage? Providing a choice? Information giving? Image making? What is this presentation supposed to do?
2   **Define the main topic**
What is the presentation about?
What are the limits of this?
What is the title?
3   **Research your audience**
Why should they listen to you?
What are their objectives?
What will they need to know to reach their objectives?
What do they already know about the topic?
What interests/frightens/concerns and turns them on?
What benefits will exactly match their needs?
What is their business background?
What is the relationship between them and your company?

4 **Select, sort and prioritize the information you will present**
What *must* they know?
What will they need to clarify their understanding?
What will illustrate your points?
What is just padding? (cut it out!)
Prioritize again in order of importance and logic.
Use the 'So what' and the 'So this means . . .' tests.

5 **Prepare the presentation**
Think about the end:
Call to action (what will fulfil your objective?)
Summary of main points and benefits.
Contact information about the presenter/company.
Think about the questions the presentation will raise in the minds of the audience.
How will you control the Q/A session?
How will you start/end the QA session?

Now prepare the start of the presentation:

How will you 'frame it up'?
How will you catch their attention?
Which concerns will you be addressing?
Why are you giving this presentation?
How will you make them listen actively?
What is your conclusion?

Now prepare the middle of the presentation:

Do you have clear and relevant examples for your main points?
What analogies, metaphors and similes will make your meaning clear and interesting?
How will you link your points together?

6 **Prepare the visuals**
What main points need illustrating?
Are there any figures or quotes that need to be put on a slide?
Is there any spatial information that needs illustrating?
Do you have a theme for your slides?
Are all your slides really necessary?
Have you prepared a title slide and is your contact information on it?

7 **Will you need handouts?**
How will these be distributed?

8 **Edit the presentation**
Is there enough proof/usefulness?
Is there enough excitement/involvement?
Is there enough detail/thinking space?
Is there enough positioning/logic?
How will you get the audience to remember this information?

9 **Rehearse**
At the very least *speak aloud* the start and the end of the presentation. Best of all rehearse in front of a critical colleague who knows your audience.

Good luck and may the equipment be with you!

4   Reports and proposals

'What I tell you three times is true.' The Bellman, *Hunting of the Snark,*
Lewis Carroll

4.1. Introduction

The essence of report and proposal writing is 'knowing your audience'. Reports and proposals are probably the most common written forms of communication found in businesses, public and private organisations and can take up a significant part of people's working lives. Both can vary significantly in size, scope and purpose, from what is little more than a glorified memo to multiple-volume tender documents for major government procurements. However, the basic principles remain the same; size is not important, and what is described here has general application. The chapter has been split into two sections, one on reports and one on proposals, in recognition of the difference between a reporting document and a selling document. Some blurring of this distinction may creep out from time to time, particularly if you take the time to study 'unbiased' reports in the light of the information included in this chapter.

4.2 Reports

Report: a document or communication presenting information on a specified subject.

This is the most common form of written work that you are likely to be involved with. Whatever your role you are going to have to write something about it at some time or another, so you may as well do it right. There are four questions which you should answer before you set pen to paper or fingers to keyboard:

- Who will read the document?
- What is the objective in writing it?
- What are the key points?
- What should the structure be?

The first of these is our old friend, 'Know your audience' – the ground that was covered in Chapters 2 and 3 on this topic still applies. However, you need to have a slightly different slant on it as you will be communicating indirectly via paper (or fax/e-mail etc.) rather than face to face. You don't have the opportunity to answer questions interactively about what you write, similarly you don't have the opportunity to change the level at which you present the information as you would in a conversation or a presentation. Consequently it is vital that you get as much information about your reader as possible. The following checklist is a starting point:

- Is English their first language?
- Are they technical/business people?
- Are they decision makers?
- What are their interests?
- What will they gain from it?
- What do they really want to know?

You need to establish what they are interested in before you do anything else, as the audience will affect your treatment of the other points above. People find it easier to understand words that they use all the time, so they are also more comfortable, and hence more receptive to the message, if it is written using those words.

The second issue concerns your objective in writing it, and it is here that some blurring of the edges between a report and a proposal can creep out. Say a strict objective was given to you, such as, write a report showing how changes in our pricing policy on breakfast cereals has affected revenue in our stores during the last six months; such a report would consist of straightforward facts and no conclusions/predictions. However, you might be asked to write a report on the sale of breakfast cereals in the stores over the last twelve months including suggestions as to how these may be improved. Here your brief is much wider.

The third point is analytical in nature. You need to look at the material you have gathered for your report and determine what is important and what is not. Finally, structure is very important. A badly constructed report may well have all the facts in it, and even have valid conclusions and recommendations, but if they are buried away in the wrong place then there is a fair chance that they will be missed.

The rule of thumb is that which was traditionally taught at school; 'say what you're going to say, say it, say what you've said.' In other words, a summary of key points first (often called a management summary), sections with the meat in the middle (relegate very detailed information to appendices if it threatens to dilute the message), and then present a conclusion at the end which ties together the facts with any recommendations.

Typical contents of a report

Introduction: Describe what the report is for, who it is aimed at, and an overview of the structure of the report and what information can be found where.

Summary: A summary of the main points of the report, preferably in the order they are presented in the main body of the document. It should also include a summary of the conclusions as well.

Main report: This may be one or several chapters/sections which present the information of the report.

Conclusion: A clear presentation of any conclusions that have been drawn, and the justification for them.

Appendices: Detailed information that supports the proposal. Technical, statistical, or legal material that would be either too long or too specialist to include with the main body of the report.

Table 4.1 shows a four-stage production plan.

Draft	Description	Purpose	Notes
First draft	A very rough draft which aims to have all the information present but is not concerned with format or literary merit.	To establish the content of each section of the report and to establish what information you have/haven't got so you know where to concentrate your efforts when producing the second draft.	It is acceptable to set an arbitrary date for completing the first draft, by definition it will be whatever has been produced by that date. You don't put the date off because you feel you could write a bit more given time.
Second draft	A complete draft of the whole document in the correct format. It should be properly written and spell checked.	To provide the basis for the delivered report – any changes to this should be editorial (not new writing) or concerned with getting the grammar right, the spelling correct and improving the visual appearance.	Within the constraints of the time available to deliver the final report the date for this draft should be set according to an estimate based on a review of the first draft – sufficient time should be made available for people to do the job well.
Customer draft	A single copy of the document from which copies will be made to supply the reports audience.	To become the master copy of the document. The only changes to this will be very minor and last-minute spelling/typographical corrections.	Copies made from this should be individually page checked to catch any collation/copying errors that creep in.
Delivered report(s)	The actual report, with as many copies as are required for its purpose.	To meet the requirements of the people/organization that commissioned the report.	No report is ever perfect, but it must be delivered eventually. Don't be too upset if you find a minor typographical error in the delivered package. The deadline for this is usually specified when the report is commissioned and cannot be changed.

**4.2.1
Drafts and proofs**

It is wise to spend time proof reading and spell checking (that's why nature gave us word processors). Obvious spelling, grammatical and formatting errors can distract from the value of a report to such an extent that the validity of the information contained is compromized.

If a document is going to be printed in large quantities then you may wish to add an additional printer's proof where you check the printed version of the document prior to the production run. It is extremely embarrassing, not to mention expensive, to have to scrap a thousand copies of a twenty-page report because the date is wrong on the first page.

**4.3
Proposals**

Proposal: A document or communication whose purpose is to persuade the reader to take a particular course of action.

The fundamental difference between a proposal and a report is its purpose: the proposal is intended to sell something, an idea, a product, a service etc., whereas a report is usually intended to pass on information in an impartial manner. Do not forget that all the points concerning the audience, objectives, key points and structure still apply to proposals.

In this chapter the proposals under consideration are business ones. However, the same principles would apply to a proposal to ask an employer to provide new staff facilities, to request the council to install traffic calming measures in a residential street, and so on.

**4.3.1
Why write proposals?**

A short answer might be 'To make money, by winning business'. Slightly more detailed reasons are to:

- Persuade the customer to buy your solution
- Define the solution you are offering
- Determine the price of what you supply
- Limit your liability.

A proposal can be an important vehicle for selling a solution. A successful proposal also provides the basis for the contract between the supplier and the customer. Proposals are only part of the selling process; some companies even try to maintain such a close relationship with the customer that they never have to write any proposals, or, at least, not until long after the sale has gone through!

In other words, the proposal has two main – and sometimes conflicting – functions; that of a sales aid and legal commitment to supply. Writing proposals is a craft where practice and experience count. However, the basics covered here will enable you to produce effective proposals almost immediately, and will provide the theoretical knowledge to enable proposals to be analysed and learnt from in the light of experience.

**4.3.2
Writing style**

A proposal should be easy to read, understand and evaluate. If it is not then you stand little chance of influencing the reader to do business with you or accept your proposition. If they can't communicate with you when you are presumably trying the hardest, how are they going to cope once they've bought from you and become 'just another customer'?

A journalist's motto states, 'Make it short, make it snappy, make it up!' The first two points are good advice to the proposal writer. Never say in half a page what you can say in half a line. The longer something is the more scope there is for misunderstanding, boredom, and irritation. The third point can be more constructively re-phrased as 'make your mind up' (about what you want to say). To make up your mind, answer the following questions:

- What do you wish to achieve?
- Who is the audience?
- Do you have all the information required?

You are a company that makes wedding videos. If you were writing a proposal to the bank for a business loan for a new video camera, your goal (what you wish to achieve) would be for the bank to lend you the money on terms acceptable to you. The audience would be the bank manager and support staff such as the bank's credit-checking agency. The information required would be the business case justifying the purchase of a new computer, such as the ability to film two weddings simultane-ously and the figures showing how the loan would be repaid from increased revenue.

Use the client's own words within your proposal whenever possible. This is a very effective way of demonstrating that you have understood what they want and have listened to them in all those meetings you had while trying to establish their needs. For example you may find that the client has frequently used particular phrases, such as 'time to market' in their conversations and correspondence with you. This gives you two messages; one is that 'time to market' (the ability to get a new product out to customers in a short time) is something that matters to them, the other is that they are comfortable with the phrase 'time to market'. By using this phrase in your proposal, providing you don't over do it, you will be talking in a language familiar to them, which will make it easier for them to understand you. It will also give the proposal a 'tone' that they are comfortable with. These two factors will make the client more likely to feel well-disposed towards your proposition than towards one that has ignored these guidelines.

If there are a large number of limitations (caveats) to the supply then make sure that they are given in such a way as not to make the whole document sound negative. By all means give them a section of their own, but don't put them in the main 'selling' part of the proposal unless they absolutely have to be there. An example of a caveat might be that the price quoted for the installation of equipment was subject to the client's premises being ready for the work to go ahead on a given date. For example, ' The price quoted for installation assumes that the customer site is ready to receive the equipment on the date agreed. This shall include provision of power and data cabling and provision of access for the delivery van and a fork-lift truck. Should this not be the case and a repeat visit has to be made then there will be an additional charge of £250 for each repeat visit.'

Style is always a matter of personal taste but there are some basics which should be observed.

- Get the spelling correct
- Ensure the grammar is accurate
- Keep sentences fairly short
- Avoid confusing analogies
- Do not introduce new ideas into conclusions
- Do have a summary at the start

- Do make sure that all the information is relevant
- Edit and proof read
- Edit and proof read again (and preferably again)

Proposal presentation

Even more so than with reports, the accuracy of the spelling, layout and format of a proposal has an important impact on its chances of success, so it is vital they are given sufficient attention. Indeed, the physical presentation of a proposal can be a major factor in getting the reader to treat it favourably from the start.

The appeal of a proposal is significantly enhanced by having it attractively bound (perhaps in a ring binder) and having good artwork on the outer cover. You might consider incorporating the 'logo' of the people who are to receive the proposal in the cover design. The proposal will also benefit from being made easy to use by having dividers in between the chapters making it simple to get straight to the section the reader is interested in. The better it looks and the easier it is to use the more likely the reader is to look favourably on the proposal, and the more likely it is to be successful.

4.3.3 Features and benefits

One of the cornerstones of proposal writing is understanding the difference between a feature and a benefit. This is easily achieved by liberal use of the 'so what' test. For example:

- Feature: This car has an efficient heater.
- Benefit: It can keep the occupants warm in cold weather enabling its use in winter.
- So what? The prospective purchaser lives in Bahrain, so he isn't bothered about a heater. (He'd prefer refrigeration.)

This is a trivial example but it is an important lesson to learn. Most systems/ solutions that are offered to a customer usually have a large number of features (such as, it can process fifty thousand transactions per second). However, what matters is whether this feature has a material or qualitative benefit to the customer.

Material, or quantifiable, benefits are those for which you can show a 'bottom line' justification. For example, if you supply a system which allows a customer to do without 10 per cent of their back-office staff because it automatically matches trades to clients then there is an obvious cost saving. This is a material benefit.

Qualitative benefits are less tangible. You might have a 'widget' that allows a dealer to see two sources of market information simultaneously on the same screen, instead of having to switch between the two. This makes the dealer's working life easier, but it might not make her more productive in any measurable way. People who sell electronic mail and office automation systems have had to become masters of the qualitative benefit; it can be done.

It is usually much easier to make a case for a material benefit than for a qualitative one. If you are dependent on qualitative benefits then take a lot of trouble to make clear what they are.

Once you have sorted out the benefits from the features, the next step is to find out which benefits are most relevant to the prospect. You do this by presenting them to the customer informally and judging the reaction. If they tell you it doesn't matter, then it is not relevant so don't stress it.

Table 4.2 Qualitative versus quantitative benefits.

Fact	Feature	Qualitative Benefit	Quantitative Benefit
Top speed of 150 m.p.h.	Fastest car on the road	Glamour and excitement	Gets you there faster and so saves time
Leather upholstery	Finest Moroccan calf	Really comfortable	Lasts longer than fabric
Metallic paintwork	6 coats of paint	Colour choice	Metallic paint no extra cost
Two-year warranty	Longest warranty offered	No worries about repair costs for two years	No repair costs for two years
45 m.p.g.	Economical fuel consumption	Fewer refuelling stops	Saves money
64-cubic-feet boot	Biggest boot in the business	Carries huge amounts of luggage	Saves having to hire another vehicle for large loads

Discussion

What are the differences between a feature and a benefit? Think of recent purchases you have made, and why you made them. How would you go about selling a qualitative benefit in a proposal? Apply the so what test to a selection of newspaper and television advertisements for products that you are likely to buy in the next twelve months.

4.3.4
Structure

If the customer has a preferred format, then use it. For example, government departments often specify a very detailed contents list together with questions that must be answered in a particular way, which enables them to compare like with like when evaluating tenders. If none is given then use the format preferred by the organization for whom you are writing the proposal. If there isn't one of those then there are some basic rules to guide you.

As with reports, 'Say what you are going to say, say it, say what you've said' is a good maxim to follow.

A skeleton structure for a proposal

Management summary: This should provide a brief outline of what is proposed and the overall cost and time table. It should also collect together the major benefits of the proposal and demonstrate the credibility (of you or your organization) of the solution.

Description of requirement: This is where you demonstrate that you understand what the problem or requirement is that you are offering a solution for. For example, by describing the background to the problem, why it is important, and what specifically needs to be done.

Possible solutions: Here you would further demonstrate your understanding, and expertise, by reviewing a number of different approaches that you might take and their relative merits. This section may be left out or merged with the next one in many cases, but it is often a simple way to show that you have thought about the requirement in depth, not just come up with something off the top of your head.

Proposed solution: This is the heart of the document. It has two functions, the first being to define the proposal in sufficient detail to make it clear what is being offered, and the second to bring out the benefits of the proposal and demonstrate that they are relevant (remember the 'so what' test).

Pricing: This should be a clear presentation of the costs (to the customer/recipient) involved in implementing the proposal and when these costs will be incurred. For example there may be a 20 per cent payment required ahead of any work starting, or there may be a discount offered for buying a particular quantity. It is vital that this section is completely unambiguous, and that the proposal makes it clear what will be obtained at what cost.

Appendices: There may be much background, technical, legal, or other detailed information which is only of specialist interest, or required only to justify points made in the main proposal. Such information tends to be lengthy and potentially difficult to read and is much better put in separate appendices where it can be referred to if necessary. Typical information you might find in appendices includes: product brochures, company accounts, statistical data, and contract details.

4.3.5 Checklist

The following checklist is based on experience, and it does work! If you can't answer all the questions, then you should think again before delivering your proposal.

Do you know what the customer wants?
Can you supply what the customer wants?
Who are the decision makers?
What is the timescale for the proposal and the project?
Do they have the money?
Who are the competitors?
Are any of them 'sitting tenants'?
Is the business worth bidding for?
What are the benefits of what you're proposing?
Are they relevant to the customer?
Have you got a plan for producing the proposal?
Are the resources available to produce the proposal?
Does the customer specify a format for the proposal? If so, have you followed it?
Have you got the proposal approved (for example, by QA/management)?
Has enough proof reading been done?
Have the printing facilities been organized?
How many copies are required?
Do you know where to send the proposal?
Are you sure you've done enough proof reading?

4.3.6 Readability

For those who don't trust their writing skills then this is a rough and ready guide to the readability of a proposal. Often word processors will do this, or something similar, for you, and many go even further. There are also many standard indexes of readability available, such as Flesch-Kincaid, Coleman-Liau and Bormuth Grade Levels. However, here is a simple method of calculating a readability index.

Divide the total numbers of words in the passage by the number of sentences (choose a few sample pages of text rather than using the whole document). Make a note of this number.

Then count the number of words with three syllables or more per 100 words (ignore capitalized words, composite words such as bookkeeper, hyphenated words such as packet-switching, and words of three syllables ending in -es or -ed which are verb forms, such as 'proposes'). Make a note of this number.

To determine the readability index add the numbers together and multiply by 0.4. If the answer is greater than 10 then the proposal is easy to read. Between 10 and 12 then it is still readable, but might be difficult for someone whose first language is not English. If the result is higher than this then it will get more and more difficult for foreigners to read. Over 16 and it is suitable only for well-educated, native English speakers.

4.4 Summary

Reports and proposals have much in common, in that they are both concerned with passing on information to a third party with some outcome in mind. In both cases the most important factor is to consider the audience – who is going to read it – and write for them.

Where the two differ most is in emphasis on selling a concept. The proposal will be geared towards making a case, overcoming possible objections to the case – highlighting strengths – demonstrating how weaknesses would be overcome. A proposal is biased towards a particular outcome. To achieve this it needs to show how the reader will benefit from following a particular course of action and that failing to take the action, or taking a different course, will be less beneficial and may even be disadvantageous. When looking at benefits the writer should make frequent use of the 'so what' test.

4.5 Exercises

4.5.1 Reports and proposals

Community action I

Write a (short) report on the problems associated with speeding in residential areas that include both schools and shops.

Community action II

Write a proposal for lowering the speed limit on a road that passes a school and a busy shopping parade.

Reports versus proposals

Compare the two and note the differences in style.

4.5.2 Features and benefits

Define what the features are of a video recorder (or a car, hifi, washing machine, mobile phone), then equate them with benefits for different potential buyers (a teacher, a student, a pensioner, a travelling sales rep).

5   Correspondence

'I can't write five words but that I change seven.' Dorothy Parker

5.1
Introduction

Correspondence is vital to business. Even in the electronic age hard-copy communication is still the norm for formal business communications – letters, memos, minutes of meetings. Hard-copy correspondence has several advantages over face-to-face or voice-to-voice linear communication. Correspondence can be re-read, pondered over at leisure, referred to as an accurate record of what was intended, promised, acted upon or reported. Hard-copy correspondence should ideally represent a clear, accurate and lasting account of what the communicator intended.

This chapter gives guidance on how to go about producing such correspondence and how to make it as effective as possible. As with many of the other forms of communication dealt with in this book the key to this chapter is 'Know your audience'.

5.2
Letters

In business, letters are used for a variety of purposes, such as providing quotations, asking for information, making complaints, answering complaints, informing candidates of interview results, and getting agreement to a change in what is being supplied. Although different purposes dictate different approaches to correspondence the basic principles are common to all. Letters have the advantage of being a permanent record of a communication which can be referred to should disagreements arise, and can be used in a court of law as evidence (a fact to bear in mind when quoting prices, listing services and making commitments to a customer). Letters are, however, a relatively expensive method of communication, as well as being time consuming to produce.

5.2.1
Format

There are many different physical formats in use for business letters – address top left, address top right, where you put the date, and so on. Contrary to what you might find in some more traditional secretarial skills courses there is no longer a 'right' way of laying out business letters. Many companies have their own standard layouts, and if you are working for a company with defined standards you will, and should, have to use them. However, there are some fundamental pieces of information that you should make sure are present on a letter as a minimum:

- The date
- Your address (with phone, fax, e-mail etc.)
- The recipient's name
- Your name
- Any specific legal requirements (such as company registration number, VAT registration number, registered charity number)
- Sender reference (this makes life easier for the reply to the letter to be dealt with speedily)
- A heading which allows the recipient to identify immediately what the letter is about.

Optionally you may wish to consider adding the customer's address (in the past this was considered essential), the customer's organization name, your job title, mobile phone number and so on.

Harking back to the 'know your audience' theme, make sure that all this information is accurate, as it will destroy any credibility that you have if you spell the recipient's name wrong.

While there are no longer precise rules for the placing of this information on the page it should be clearly and cleanly arranged so that the recipient does not require the detective skills of Sherlock Holmes to work out where the letter came from and who to get in touch with regarding it.

5.2.2
Envelopes

There are three things that must be on an envelope – the recipient's name, role and address (including the name of the organization or company). Optionally you may include your organization's name and address, providing you don't place it so that it confuses the postal service. In practice many organizations have pre-printed envelopes with their own logo on the front and a return address on the back.

Again, it is very important that you get the information on the envelope correct, both in content and spelling. For example, someone who is the Managing Director of a company will not be well disposed to receive something addressed to the 'Sales Manager'. Again, consider your audience.

5.2.3
Forms of address

As with format, today the rules governing forms of address have been considerably relaxed. It is rare to send letters starting 'Dear Sir'. Many letters use forenames as a matter of course. The concept of familiarity today is quite the reverse of what it was in the 1950s and before. Then it was an indication that you knew someone very well indeed if you used their first name. Today, you are more likely to know their first name than their surname. A typical modern business letter may well commence with something like 'Dear Helen' and end with 'Regards'.

However, some people and organizations do still adopt more formal approaches and when dealing with them you should do the same – at least if you don't want to cause unnecessary ill-feeling. We have only covered the basics, the archaic, your obedient servant etc. has been left as a research

Table 5.1

Beginning	Ending
Dear Sir	Yours faithfully
Dear Mr/Mrs/Miss/Ms/Dr	Yours sincerely
Dear Harry/Sally etc.	Regards
Dear Harry/Sally (closer acquaintance)	Best wishes, or Kind regards

project for those interested in historical study. Table 5.1 pairs up the commonest variants.

When writing to people with formal qualifications, such as Dr (Doctor), Professor, and so forth it is normal to include this title. For example Dear Dr Smith, Dear Professor Higgins, the associated ending would still be sincerely, regards, best wishes or kind regards, depending on how well you know the recipient of the letter.

Those who find themselves dealing with people with formal titles (peer of the realm, members of parliament, members of the armed services etc.) should look up the appropriate form of address, in books such as *Debrett's Correct Form* (1992) or *Titles and Forms of Address* (1990).

Discussion

Why is it important to get the right form of address on a letter? How might you assess what is appropriate for a particular individual?

Where could you find out the correct spelling of people's names, their correct job title and address?

**5.2.4
Structure**

Letters need structure in order to convey information effectively. It is no use just writing down ideas as they come off the top of your head, as what will result will tend to be confusing and illogically constructed. Much of what was covered in Chapter 4 concerning structure and content applies equally to letters. You need to introduce what the letter is about, present the information that you need to support your case or request, and then provide a summary which includes clear information on what you want the reader to do next. It is normal practice to cover only one topic in a single paragraph to reduce the chances of confusion.

An example of an introduction might be, 'At the last progress meeting we were actioned to send you an up-to-date statement of the charges that your company has incurred to date. Please find the enclosed . . .'

A main paragraph might go along the following lines, 'Although the kitchen equipment will be delivered to your premises a week later than was originally planned there will be no change to the completion date for the refurbishment of your restaurant. We have been able to bring forward the decoration of the dining area so that it will take place in the time when we would have been installing the ovens.'

An example closing paragraph, 'Should you have any questions concerning this please contact me on 0123–456789. The enclosed map will show you how to get to us and I look forward to seeing you on 25 August.'

To summarize, a business letter needs to contain:

- *Introduction* Often just a reminder of the matter in hand.
- *Main paragraphs* What you want done, information you need to pass on etc.
- *Closing paragraph* Saying goodbye, stating how to get in touch with you, calls for action etc.

5.2.5
Typical business
letter

The House
2 Newtown Road
Someplace
AB1 7CD

01234–56789

17 May 1995

Dear Caroline

Please find the enclosed, signed contract, for the *Made Simple Business Communications book* (or whatever we end up calling it!). I think it is all very exciting. It will be wonderful to see it when it is published.

Please also find the enclosed map of how to find us on Wednesday 24 May, at 3:00 p.m. I'm looking forward to meeting you again and will put the kettle on in good time.

If you need to get in touch before then, or if you have any problems finding us just call on 01234–56789 or fax us on 01234–98765.

Very best wishes,

David Nickson

5.2.6
Use of postscripts

Postscripts really belong to the days before word processors and personal computers. Their original function was to add new information that occurred to you after the letter had been hand-written or typed. As there existed no facility to edit text once it was committed to paper the only way to change it was either to write the whole thing out again or to add additional information at the end of the letter. This latter approach is known as a postscript – from the Latin, *post scriptum*, abbreviated to p.s., meaning 'after writing'. Technology has made the postscript non-essential as you can simply edit the existing text and reprint as needed. That said, the postscript has a useful function as a means of including information not relevant to the main body of the letter or as a place to include a personal message that would not be appropriate elsewhere.

For example, 'P.s. How did the exhibition go?' might be added to the end of a letter about renewing a contract with someone you have been trading with for some time. It is not relevant to the letter but it is a genuine request for information.

5.3
Memos

Within most organizations internal written communication takes the form of the memo. Memos are typically short and to the point – it is unusual for them to cover more than two pages – most are one or two paragraphs long. They are used to convey a wide range of information, from a reminder about not dropping litter in the corridors to highly confidential information on the company's current financial status, disciplinary action against individual staff and so on.

5.3.1
Style

The style and language for memos require careful consideration. Not only must you consider the audience for whom you are writing, but you must also consider who else might see it. Once you have committed your views to paper they provide an audit trail of what you did/did not say. Memos exist to convey information efficiently and quickly so your goal is to get as much information in as few words as possible, providing the meaning is still clear. Consequently the style that you use is going to be determined by the combination of these two requirements: audience/function and clear/concise. A sanity check on the quality of a memo is to read it as if it were addressed to you and then ask yourself: did you understand it? Did it convey a positive message?

5.3.2
Structure

The subject of the memo should provide the equivalent of an introduction in a larger document, then the subject matter should be presented, finally any responses required must be clearly made, preferably at the end of the memo. In some cases this will be easily achieved in a single paragraph:

'Will all staff please note that the canteen will be closed on Friday 13th this month for the installation of a new cooking range. As an alternative, Earls the Caterers will operate a 'delivered to your desk' sandwich service. The range of sandwiches will be pinned up on the notice board and you should phone your order in to them on extension 3456 before 11:00 on Friday. Should you have any special dietary requirements please call them on the same number no later than 16:30 on Thursday.'

In other cases the memo may run to several paragraphs following a similar structure to a small report (see also Chapter 4).

The physical format of a memo will vary from organization to organization, but there will normally be some standard, possibly including the organization's logo, which should be followed. The example given here is typical of such a format.

Interoffice Memo

To:	Suzy Siddons
From:	David Nickson
Date:	24 October 1995
Subject:	Exercises for *Made Simple* book

CC: Caroline Struthers

Suzy

Please can you let me know when you will be able to deliver a draft of the exercise for the Negotiation Chapter. Ideally we need to get a complete draft of this chapter to Caroline by Wednesday 28th November. If you can't manage this please can you let me know ASAP so that we can re-schedule the next progress meeting accordingly.

Regards

David

Discussion

How are memos different from letters? Discuss the different approaches you would take in writing memos to people you work closely with and memos sent out to a wider audience, for example informing the whole organization of a change of fire regulations.

5.4
Meeting minutes

Some meetings, such as project progress meetings, business reviews, formal customer meetings, have to be minuted. The reason for this is to make sure that there is a permanent record of what was agreed and what action people undertook to do. This record can then be used to measure progress and ensure that there is a common understanding of what is to happen and what has happened.

The starting point for any set of minutes is that they should indicate who was at the meeting, where and when it was. Next they should be used to record any key facts and who supplied them, and the resolution of any debates. Note that it is usually unnecessary to record everything that was said or how decisions were reached. However, there will be occasions where one, or more, people at a meeting will wish to formally state their disagreement with a majority decision. In this case they may ask that their point of view be minuted to show that they were of a different opinion to the group.

The other key function of minutes is to record who has committed to do what, normally referred to as 'actions'. When recording actions in minutes it is normal to adopt some form of abbreviated notation to link the actions with the meeting and the individual(s) concerned. For example, an action taken at a meeting held on the 7 July 1995 for David Nickson to do something might be identified as 07/07/95-DN-1/1. The 1/1 showing that it was the first action given at the first meeting. This provides a valuable means of tracking progress against the actions. It also makes it visually clear which actions are out-standing and from how long ago. If you are having your tenth meeting and there is an outstanding action labelled 08/08/95-DN-2/1 then you know that there is a problem with this action and that it should be actively reviewed.

It is not always essential to incorporate the date in an action identifier – the meeting number may suffice and makes for shorter references. However, it can be an advantage to have the date there to make it readily apparent how much time has passed since the action was placed.

Minutes of the Third New Business Marketing Meeting

Meeting held at Headquarters, Bracknell

Date 21/06/95   Time 11:00 hours

Present: Tallulah Bankhead, John Betjeman, Clara Bow (Chairperson), Jean Harlow, Ogden Nash (Secretary)

Apologies for absence: Margaret Rutherford, Bill Wordsworth

1 **Minutes of last meeting**
   These were accepted as being a true and accurate record of the previous meeting and were duly signed by the secretary.

2 **Matters arising**
   There were none.

3 **Review of actions**
   Re action 12/05/95/CB-3

   CB stated that she would not be available for any more public appearances as part of the 'IT Girl' campaign promoting Information Technology for women, owing to other commitments.

   JH was tasked with finding a replacement.

   Action 21/06/95/JH-3/1

4 **New business**

   ON stated that a quotation had been requested from the Honey Marketing Company for an advertisement with a wildlife theme. Something involving owls and cats was being produced for consideration.

5 **Any other business**

   JB asked that the reception area in the building have a full-time receptionist as his office was on the top floor of the building and he did not like being continually summoned by bells when reception was unattended.

6 **Next meeting**

   The next meeting was scheduled to be held at 12:00 on 4 July 1995, in the Poets' Room at the Odeon building, London.

   The agenda to be unchanged.

It is important to have a formal agenda for any meeting which is to be minuted. The agenda will provide the structure for the minutes. This is in addition to the other benefits that arise from having meeting agendas in terms of control and direction of the meeting.

Discussion	Why is it important that minutes are agreed at the start of the next meeting? Consider the statement 'Minute-taking is power'.

5.5 Summary

Correspondence is of considerable importance in all organizations. Correspondence with the outside world has a major impact on the image of the company that sends it out, so it is important to get it right. Internal correspondence – memos, minutes of meetings for example – needs to be clear and concise if the overall efficiency of the organization is not to be compromized. Similarly, internal correspondence needs to be carefully worded to ensure that it conveys a positive message to the recipients. What you write and how you present it will have a significant impact on how you are perceived by others.

5.6 Exercises

5.6.1 Letters

Sales copy

You are a sales representative with a company that produces air-conditioning equipment. There is a new managing director, Rupert Brook, at your best customer, Poets' Corner Ltd. Write a letter introducing yourself to him with a view to arranging a meeting so that you can explain your company's product range.

Accountancy

You work in accounts and are writing to a supplier, Schrodinger Catalytic Supplies Ltd., 2 Heisenberg Avenue, Newtown, AB1 2CD. You need them to clarify uncertainty relating to an invoice they have sent you – it is not clear if it is for three converters at £250 or for two converters at £350. The total amount is correct but you need to tie it in with the stock control system before you can authorize payment. The name of your contact at Schrodingers is Dr Feynman.

5.6.2 Memo

Staff announcement

You have just negotiated a staff discount of 10 per cent on goods with the local fashion store, Lana Lang Limited, Sunset Boulevard, Cleethorps, AB1 2CD. Write a memo to all the people in your organization explaining the terms of the discount and explaining to them that they must have their ID card with them to claim the discount.

Leave of absence

Write a memo to your manager explaining who will cover for you while you are on the 'Your Number Is Up' training course on basic accounting skills. The course lasts three days and you will not be contactable for its duration.

5.6.3 Minutes

Organize a meeting with colleagues, fellow students, friends or anyone else you can persuade to join in. Agree who is to be the Chair (see also Chapter 11, Working in Teams) of the meeting and invent an agenda, anything that interests you. Take notes of the meeting and produce minutes of it a week later. Ask the other people who were present to comment on how well the minutes report what actually happened (as they remember it!) and the clarity of the information presented. If you like you can run follow up meetings with different people taking the minutes, chairing the meeting etc.

'Along the electric wire the message came, things are no better they are much the same'. Attributed to Poet Laureate Alfred Austin on the illness of Edward VII.

E-mail: System by which electronic messages take the place of paper-based, facsimile and some telephone communications both within an organization or group and with the world outside the organization or group.

6.1 Introduction

In many organizations electronic mail, or e-mail as it is more popularly known, has taken over from the internal memo, minutes of meetings, invitations to meetings, some telephone calls, and even those sticky-back notelets people leave on your computer screen when you're away from your desk. Although the function of these communications remains much the same as was described in Chapter 5, e-mail has a personality and peculiarities of its own which make it worthy of study in its own right.

6.1.1 Glossary

Because e-mail has aspects of specialist technology associated with it there are a number of 'jargon' words which may need clarifying, so we have put together the following glossary.

Audit trail	A record of events which allows the sender/receiver of an e-mail to know when it was sent, when it was read, by whom etc.
Back-up	A copy of data, in this case and e-mail, made to provide security against computer system failures, theft, fire etc. These may be kept in the same location or, better, on a separate location to the original information.
Blind copies	Copies of mail messages which are sent to one or more people without the other recipients of the message knowing about it.
Bulletin board	An electronic system where messages can be left/retrieved using a computer and a modem. Basis of early e-mail systems. Bulletin boards often cater for special interest groups, for example anglers, cooks, film enthusiasts.
Buttons	Pictorial representations of 'buttons' on a computer screen which can be 'pressed' by keyboard or point device (for example a mouse) action to activate a function of an e-mail system.

Compuserve	A commercial network provider – includes e-mail and Internet access and various special interest groups.
Data compression	Technique for reducing the amount of space the information contained in a file needs to occupy – thus speeding its transmission over a network and reducing the amount of file space needed to store it.
Directory	Structure in which files are stored. Used for organizing information for convenient retrieval.
E-mail	Shorthand for 'electronic mail'.
Encryption	Method by which messages can be coded to make them difficult to read by unauthorized recipients.
Fax	Facsimile transmission whereby documents are transmitted over the telephone network. Some e-mail systems make use of fax modems to send e-mail messages directly to fax machines.
Fax modem	Device for sending/receiving computer data and facsimile data over telephone networks.
File	A collection of related information – for example a single e-mail message.
Folder	An electronic equivalent of a folder in a filing cabinet, used for storing e-mails.
Internet	An international data network, often used for sending and sharing information on a world wide basis. Dates back to a 1970s United States Department of Defence network providing a system of communication designed to survive nuclear attack.
Mailing list	Pre-defined list which contains the e-mail addresses of a group of people.
Menu	A list of actions/choices from which the e-mail user can choose to perform particular jobs.
Modem	A device for sending computer data over a telephone line (short for MODulator, DEModulator).
Mouse	A pointing device which provides the user with the ability to move some form of pointer around a computer screen. The mouse allows particular functions of the e-mail system to be selected from 'buttons' and 'menus'. So called because of their shape and their tail – the cable connecting them to the computer system.
Netiquette	Network Etiquette. Dos and don'ts that apply within a particular network/e -mail environment. Defined by the users by common practice.

Network	A communication infrastructure that allows a group of computers, printers and other devices to exchange information and share resources.
Teleconferencing	Sound/vision/text interaction between a number of individuals over a computer network. Members of a teleconference can see and hear each other and can communicate via their keyboard/transferring data files etc.
Voice box	A location used for storing voice mail messages for a particular individual/organization. It is operated in much the same way as an answerphone system.
Voice mail	Electronic mail system which allows messages to be entered into the system via a microphone in much the same way as a dictating machine or tape recorder is used. These are then sent in the same way as ordinary e-mails.

**6.1.2
Features of e-mail
systems**

Figure 6.1 shows a typical e-mail screen (© the Microsoft Corporation) from a commonly used e-mail system. In this example you can see electronic folders for storing mail received and mail sent and temporary storage for mail that is to be deleted. There are buttons that can be activated to allow mail to be created, forwarded or replied to. In addition you can see that this particular mail system has facilities built into it for sending fax (facsimile) messages. Most mail systems will provide similar facilities, the essence of a mail system being the ability to send, receive and file information. In addition many systems provide facilities to allow users to send computer files as attachments to messages. This is very useful if you have a draft document that you wish people to comment upon, removing the need for

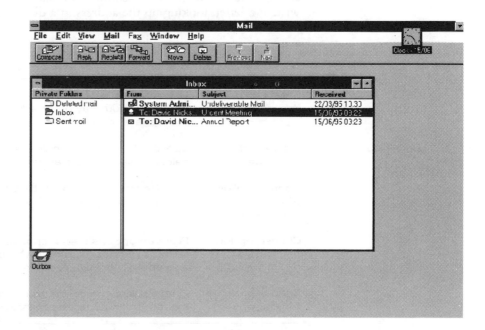

Figure 6.1 A typical e-mail system © Microsoft Corporation

large amounts of photocopying of printed documents. Most systems also provide some form of directory where you can list the mail addresses of the people you need to contact and can manage mailing lists, such as for your department, to save you from having to key-in large numbers of individual addresses.

Other common facilities within e-mail systems include the facility to change the priority of messages; high priority messages get sent faster and are flagged as being urgent to the recipient by being in a different colour or some similar visual cue. You can also send messages by the equivalent of registered post; once the recipient has read the message you receive an e-mail telling you that they have done so, and when. This can be a significant benefit when dealing with urgent matters. E-mail can provide the benefits and responsibilities of an audit trail, which makes it the ideal solution to those 'You didn't tell me', 'Oh yes I did' arguments.

6.1.3.
Sending an e-mail

Although different e-mail systems have slightly different interfaces and different ways of doing things there are common elements involved in sending, or receiving, an e-mail message. Table 6.1 provides a typical list of actions you might follow in sending an e-mail. The steps are analogous to writing a letter, looking up the address in a diary, addressing the envelope,

Table 6.1

Create text of the message	Use a simple text editor to enter the text of the message. You may be able to spellcheck the message at this stage.
Address the message	Specify the person/people the mail is to be sent to, select a mailing list if appropriate.
Confirm validity of the addresses	Get the system to check that the addressees exist, and that you have not misspelled them.
Choose options	From an options menu, choose options for the e-mail such as priority (high or low), confidentiality (private, encrypted, normal), recorded delivery etc.
Send the message	Finally select the option from the menu on the system to transmit the message.

choosing what class of mail you wish to send it by and putting it in the post box.

The above makes the whole process seem vastly more laborious than it actually is. In practice it will only take seconds to minutes to create and send an e-mail.

6.1.4
Benefits of e-mail

E-mail is fast replacing, and in many organisations already has replaced, a variety of written communications that would have been sent by photo-copied documents through internal/external post – typically memos, minutes of meetings, short reports, and work requests. In addition e-mail is supplanting the telephone for some communications. It is often easier to send an e-mail than to phone several times because someone is away from their desk and has forgotten to divert their phone. The one restriction is that, to be effective, everyone in an organization, or self-contained operating unit, must be on the e-mail system. If they are not then the difficulties caused by having to remember who is and is not on the system will cause the system to fall into disuse. This means that the technology infrastructure, including access terminals and communications links, has to be in place. In addition everyone must know how to use it, which usually implies a training programme.

There are two main benefits: reduction in the use of paper, and speed of distribution of information. Both of these produce cost reductions in terms of time and materials. However, the speed of distribution of information may also lead to better-informed decision making and other indirect benefits to the organization such as the ability to send out updates very close to the time of a meeting, thus saving time at the meeting.

Furthermore, e-mail can be connected to the outside world, allowing organisations to be linked together across both corporate and geographical boundaries. This provides cost and time savings when compared with more traditional methods.

Discussion

What are the major benefits of having an e-mail system within an organization? What do you think are the prerequisites for having an effective e-mail system? How might the introduction of an e-mail system change people's ways of working and how would you go about making this effective?

6.2
Writing style

6.2.1
Effncy vs Snse

Once upon a time there was a very good manager (they do exist) who only had one shortcoming. Her e-mails were written in the same language as those advertisements that have been used for shorthand training courses; 'If u cn rd ths u cn lrn shthnd nd bcum a scrty nd gt a gd jb!' she thought that by typing in this sort of condensed English, it would save time, and the whole point of e-mail is efficiency, isn't it? Well, yes and no. The purpose of e-mail, like writing or phoning, is communication and it is arguable as to whether this practice was effective. Even if it saved her time it took each recipient some time to translate it before they understood it, and if the e-mail was sent to more than one person the time saved was probably outweighed by time wasted.

Rather than adopt the arcane shorthand of my ex-project manager you can save yourself considerable time by setting up template messages for such things as arranging meetings, and standard memos. This is much like the templates that come with WP packages even just having your name, telephone number and return e-mail pre programmed will save you that much typing. Similarly, managing distribution lists, for example your project team, your management, the people you pub with on Fridays etc. will save significant keying time. After all, when you think about it probably 50 per cent of the keystrokes in a typical e-mail are probably the same as in the last one you sent to that person, so the savings can be significant.

So what do you need to do to make e-mail communication effective? Like all other communication methods the answer is the same. Know your audience. You need to make your message readily understood and relevant to the recipient. It is no use sending someone vast screeds of material about audit trails and journaling when all they want to know is when the accounts system is going to be on-line again so they can print out their pay cheque. Despite my criticism of unnecessary shorthand it is true to say that brevity is a virtue. You should be short and to the point; if you can get your message across in a single screen it is much more likely to be successful than if the reader has to page through large amounts of information to get the idea. Most e-mail systems give you a subject field to fill in, so make use of this as an attention getter so that your e-mail stands out from the rest. For example, 'Minutes of Progress Meeting' 10/09/94 is not going to get read as quickly as 'Project Deadline Rescheduled'.

Discussion

Given an e-mail system that allowed you to set the priorities of sent mail as 'normal', 'high', 'urgent', had an option for 'registered' mail and allowed you to have a subject title that was 36 characters long, how might you deal with the following e-mails? A routine memo detailing changes to company pension scheme; an invitation to the office New Year party; a short-notice change in travel plans due to industrial action; asking for a project review meeting; and informing staff of your new phone extension number. How does this compare with traditional paper-based communication systems?

6.3
E-mail etiquette

6.3.1
Send in anger, repent at leisure

Think twice before sending an e-mail in anger. With a memo you have to have it printed and have the chance to read and reflect before telling the MD that you think your manager is not only several sandwiches but a whole hamper short of a picnic (copied to the corporate mailing list). With e-mail, once you press that send button that is it. Perhaps the old adage should become 'count to ten in binary before you e-mail in anger'. It is your prospects that are at stake. Having seen the use that some people have made of internal bulletin boards, which are available to the management, we feel that the scope of this advice might be extended to include them as well.

Another factor to keep in mind is confidentiality. A false assumption that many people make is that they think that e-mail is like a letter – confidential between them and the recipient. The truth is that it is at least open to the dreaded 'sysops' (system operators) and possibly open to a wider audience. At a financial site we recently saw this at its most embarrassing. The Help Desk people were all clustered round a terminal so we thought something good must have happened – maybe they'd found a really neat way of using X25? Actually they'd found the journal entry for a message from Steve to Sylvia detailing his views on her attributes, and would they be getting together for coffee at 10:45 as usual? Half the company was there in the coffee room to see what was on offer! Apart from mini squidgey-gates of this kind it behoves you to think of the consequences of what you put in an e-mail; you may find your erudite character analysis of your manager finding its way into a much wider circulation than you planned.

In particular you should bear in mind the use of blind copies. Many e-mail systems have a facility whereby you can have a copy sent to someone without the recipient knowing about it. I call this the paranoia option. It is bad enough when you receive an e-mail that has been copied to the IT Director, a common ploy among backside-covering e-mailers and intimidatory memo writers alike, but it is even worse not to know who else knows what you thought was a private conversation. When using this option remember that the blind copy may well be leaked by the recipient.

Discussion

How you might implement a security policy for e-mail within an organization? What are the risks to companies from e-mail systems that are connected to the outside world?

6.3.2
Print and be damned

Another confidentiality factor comes from the ability of people to print their e-mail, whereupon it becomes another readily available document to the prying eyes of people who always make a point of reading anything left on view on the top of someone's desk. This is a particular risk where old-style managers, many of whom are in their twenties – age is not always an indicator – who have their secretary print off their e-mails so they can read them and claim bogus status from never having to deal with technology. After all, they don't use the photocopier themselves, so why should they type? This means that not only are paper copies about but also that secretaries and administrative staff have free access to your thoughts and can share them with whomsoever they wish!

Corporate e-mail etiquette should also be considered. You may well find that there are standard 'shorthand' phrases that are in use all the time. You will find that using them will make communications that much easier. It is really just the same as learning the company speak, or jargon, that develops in any closed society. It is just that in e-mail it seems to be strongly pronounced and ignoring it will make you seem an outsider and raise artificial barriers to communication. Rather like when learning the etiquette that exists on bulletin boards, you need to sit on the sidelines and learn the form for yourself before you start copying the world with your messages.

Bulletin board

This is an electronic noticeboard where you can leave messages or read messages. These systems typically have a shorthand language of their own. There are strict codes of behaviour that need to be observed when using such systems. For example, many special-interest bulletin boards do not allow commercial advertising. This is policed by snowing the offender with huge amounts of junk e-mail so that they drown in a mass of messages. Similarly there are often special FAQ files (Frequently Asked Questions) that contain the answers to the most common questions relating to a particular subject. It is expected that newcomers to the system (known as newbies) read these before asking the same questions themselves. Those who fail to do this may well get 'flamed', that is, deluged in abusive mail messages. The newcomer is advised to wait and watch for a while, or get advice from an experienced user before entering into the fray themselves.

6.3.3
Check your mail

Like any system e-mail can only be as good as the people who use it. The e-mail system may deliver a message halfway across the world within a couple of minutes but if the person receiving it doesn't check their mailbox for a couple of days then it might as well have gone by carrier pigeon. It is up to the user to check their own mail and most companies will have some internal standards as to how often this must be done. If you are concerned that an urgent mail message might be ignored then you can usually choose options to send you a message to say that it has been received and read and you can mark it as being high priority. One of the benefits of e-mail is that it does provide an audit trail of what has been sent and received so important information can be tracked.

6.3.4
Managing your e-mail

There are two factors to be considered when managing your e-mail – organization for rapid access, and deleting old mail.

Filing mail

The same rules apply to organizing your e-mail as you would expect to apply to any other correspondence. You need to decide where you file the information so that you can access it quickly and conveniently. Most e-mail systems allow you to create your own filing system to suit what you are doing. Figure 6.2 shows a very simple set of folders in an e-mail system – InBox for new mail, Sent for outgoing mail, Meetings for information concerning meetings (with two 'sub-directories' for meetings about publishing, marketing and sales), Proposals and so on.

Deleting mail

Deleting old mail is very important. Failure to delete unnecessary items can result in the entire system being filled up with redundant information. This can lead to the system giving out messages such as 'Unable to create new

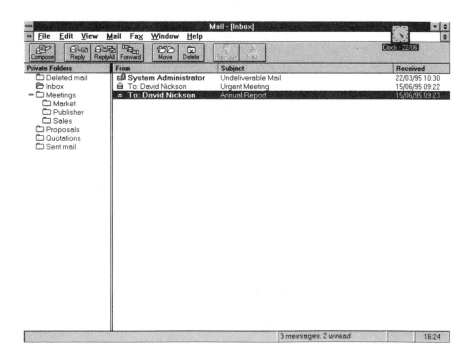

Figure 6.2 E-mail folders © Microsoft Corporation

mail, lack of disk space on server', as once the system is full it will not allow any more information to be put into it. Most organizations have policies on the use of e-mail, and if necessary will periodically delete mail older than a certain date. Anyone using an e-mail system can help by being self disciplined about what they leave on the system. The e-mail informing you of the location of Mavis's leaving drink is not going to be of any use to you once the sad event has taken place – delete it. Many e-mail systems have a facility for saving e-mails on your own personal computer, allowing you to delete them off the central system even when you need to keep them on a long-term basis. It is in your own interest to make sure that the system does not become full up – it will always fail at the time when you really do have an urgent need for the service.

6.4 Advanced technology features

More and more e-mail systems have advanced technology either built into them, or have the ability to have facilities added on later. At the time of writing, advanced features such as the ability to include voice messages and still/moving video images are available in many products but the supporting technology, such as the ability to transfer and store the large amounts of information needed to represent a television picture are still too expensive for many organisations to justify. However, voice mail is sufficiently affordable to be relatively common, and the following comments apply.

● Voice mail messages have the same security and confidentiality issues as e-mail – what you say may be heard by more than just the intended audience.
● Don't speak in anger and repent at leisure – make sure that what you say is what you want to be heard.
● Voice mail takes up a significant amount of space on the systems supporting the e-mail, so delete messages once you have heard them, or copy them off the system onto some form of back-up storage system.

Many mobile phone systems also offer voice mail (sometimes known as a voice-box) facility for leaving messages when the phone is turned off or engaged. The same points apply to this as to voice clips within e-mail.

Another facility that is rapidly becoming commonplace is the integration of e-mail with diary management systems. In such systems you schedule a meeting by specifying the date and place that you wish it to happen on and then adding an e-mail saying what the meeting is for etc. The system then puts provisional entries in people's electronic diaries and sends the e-mail with a request for confirmation of attendance. This has significant benefits in time saving when planning a meeting, and gives people the opportunity to ask e-mail questions of clarification before the meeting takes place. This latter point should make the meeting itself more productive than normal.

For the academically curious, Table 6.4 shows the relative amounts of information, showing that the difference between simple electronic messages and real-time, full-screen, colour video is immense. Data compression techniques can significantly reduce the amount of data needed to transmit a picture because much of the information is the same. That said, the difference is between sending one unit of information in a minute or so and tens of thousands of units in a second. E-mail will be significantly more economical to use than video mail for some time to come.

Table 6.4

Item description	Number of characters	Relative size	Maximum time for delivery
Typed memo	2,000	2	Minutes/hours
E-mail	1,000	1	Minutes
Word-processed document (1 page)	10,000	10	Minutes/hours
Voice-clip (30 Seconds)	300,000	300	30 seconds
Video-clip (1/5th screen, 10 seconds, 16 frames per second 256 colours)	1,600,000	1,600	10 seconds
Video-clip (full screen, 10 Seconds 24 frames per second, 256 colours)	76,800,000	76,800	10 seconds

Discussion

What has to be taken into account when looking at the economics of using e-mail systems in a business? How might the costs of e-mail be set off by benefits, in direct costs, ecological benefits, and as a consequence of more effective communications within the company? What effect might improved data-compression techniques have on the use of e-mail?

6.5 E-mail and the outside world

6.5.1 Networking the network

One of the benefits of e-mail is being able to keep in touch. Many companies are now linked to international networks such as Compuserve, Internet and national ones such as CIX. It can be a real benefit to keep in touch with people you have worked with in the past. Not just with friends – I never tire of gossiping about people I know, even if I haven't seen them for a couple of years – but with possible job and business opportunities. It is not uncommon for vacancies to be advertised on e-mail systems. Telephone companies may say it's nice to talk, but it is even nicer to write, particularly when you are spared the taste of envelope glue!

E-mail also crosses national boundaries which makes keeping in touch overseas vastly more convenient than air mail. It is faster and cheaper too! Even Concorde is no match for the Internet. What is more, some networks have facilities for originating faxes and surface mail in overseas countries at a fraction of the price of doing so by conventional methods. They do this by forwarding the message to a computer in the target country and then sending the message out using a local fax modem, thus incurring only a local phonecall charge rather than an international one. So you can even contact people who are not on e-mail services themselves.

Discussion

Discuss the implications of international e-mail services for post and telecommunications organizations in terms of profitability and levels of employment. In addition, discuss how not having access to a personal e-mail service could affect people's ability to gain employment and have access to information generally.

6.6 Summary

E-mail systems can be used instead of paper-based and some telephone communications both inside and outside an organization. Typical applications include:

- Memos
- Minutes of meetings
- Reports
- Requests for meetings
- Urgent notes
- Fax
- International post

The benefits of e-mail include:

- Speed of communication
- Cost savings
- Registered mail
- Communication across corporate, political and geographic boundaries

Prerequisites for successful e-mail include:

- Everyone you need to communicate with must be on it
- The technology infrastructure must be there to support it
- Everyone must know how to use it

7   Interviews and appraisals

'*By our first strange and fatal interview.*' John Donne, Elegy no. 16, On his mistress

7.1 Introduction

These are two of the most intensive face-to-face communication sessions you are likely to encounter as a business person, one at the beginning (hopefully) of a job and the other within the job. They are both occasions where you will be in a high-stress situation (as the interviewee/appraisee) talking about yourself, your skills, your competencies and your performance, and, as interviewer/appraiser, in a vital business process, discussing, evaluating, choosing, making plans and motivating. Both situations are intensely personal (at least on the part of the interviewee and appraisee), potentially job threatening and require a high level of communication skill.

It is important to remember that, as we said in Chapter 2, assumptions are unexploded bombs.

7.2 The job interviewing process

Recruiting a new member of your staff is likely to be the most expensive decision you will make as a manager. Do it right and you can make a fortune for your company. Do it wrong and you have an ongoing problem that will follow you for months if not years.

Most managers inherit a team of workers who know, at the very least, what they are supposed to do, who know something about your company, something about the way your team works, something about your customers, both internal and external, and something about the business processes within your department. So what happens when you bring an outsider in to this relatively stable situation?

Here are some of the possible outcomes if you do it wrong:

- You and your staff spend absolutely ages helping the new team member to get started.
- Your team norms are threatened and possibly changed, with the result that everyone examines their navels and becomes less profitable.

- The new employee is disoriented with the changes that are happening in his/her life and takes a long time to become productive.
- You discover that the perfect qualifications on the new employee's CV are no more than hype, and that the skill level you hoped for is not actually there.
- You discover that you didn't actually need your new employee to do the job they were recruited for, that the actual job has gone away and you now have a new team member who doesn't know what to do, and what's more, you don't know what on earth to do with him/her!
- You discover that your new employee simply doesn't fit into your existing team.
- You discover that your new employee is a crook.
- You never, ever, want to recruit anyone again.

Would it not be better to use a recruitment process that would avoid most, if not all, of the possibly horrible consequences of recruiting an outsider into your inside team, and the outcomes of your recruitment process were these:

- You and your staff found it an excellent exercise in efficient team working to bring a new member on board.
- Your team norms were comfortably re-assessed and strengthened by the addition of a new member.
- Your new employee's natural disorientation with the changes in her/his life were minimized by careful briefing and she/he became productive rapidly.
- The qualifications on your new employee's CV were all they were set out to be.
- Your new employee's job is exactly as described and you now have a new team member who is really filling a need.
- Your new employee fits into your existing team.
- Your new employee has all the ethics of the rest of your team.
- You look forward to recruiting more, and even more successful team members.

7.2.1
The recruitment process

Table 7.1 Looks at the recruitment process from both sides.

Interviewee	Process	Interviewer
Decide what sort of a job you want, and why you want it. Do some research: What is available, what does a job like this need in terms of skills, experience, physical capabilities? Do I have these? What do jobs like this pay? Talk to people who do the same sort of job.	Job advertisement	What exactly is the job you are advertising? Why is this job needed? Do you have a job description? What sort of a person do you want for this job? Establish the criteria that you are going to use to select the right person for the job. You need to

Table 7.1 (continued)

Interviewee	Process	Interviewer
Start looking for vacancies – in the papers, through agencies, through a network of friends. Check that you have people who will act as referees and that they have agreed to this. When you decide to apply for a job, try to find out all you can about the organization offering the job (local library, local papers, trade journals etc.) This is the *aiming* stage of the interview communication cycle	Job advertisement (continued)	define the requirements for the job in terms of the skills, attitudes, personal preferences of the ideal candidate. Then you decide on relative weights of the criteria established to build a model upon which to base the interview and the job specification for use by human resources, the agency or whoever is going to find the candidates for you. This is the *aiming* stage of the interview communication cycle
CV should contain: Essential information; professional skills, personal skills, technical skills, previous customers/employers and other relevant information. Some general points include: ● 2 to 3 pages long ● Desk-top published if possible ● Essential information first (name, age, address, qualifications, availability) ● Work history (most recent first, then work back) ● Easy to photocopy (beware of colour pictures)	Curriculum vitae	You will now probably receive a fair number of CVs for consideration. This is where the criteria that you drew up earlier come in handy; you score the CVs against them and select the three or four (at most) that are the closest match. You will, of course, have ditched all the ones that are illegible copies, impenetrably organised, and so on.
If the job advertisement asks for specific information, make sure that you include it. Make sure that you are absolutely honest about everything you put into a CV. Think about how to make your CV stand out – but no gimmicks – a businesslike approach works best. This is the first direct communication in the interview cycle, so you need to make the best impression you can.	CVs	Looking at these short listed CVs in greater detail will allow you to get some idea about the candidates. Have they got far to travel? What are their apparent strengths and weaknesses *vis-à-vis* the job? References? This, in conjunction with your selection criteria and job specification, should allow you to prepare some specific questions prior to the interview.

Table 7.1 (continued)

Interviewee	Process	Interviewer
What will you wear? (Business suits are best for men and women). How will you get there on time? (If early, you can have a look at the surroundings and decide whether you like them or not). What do you need to take? (diplomas, references, examples of your work?) What do you want to know about the job itself and the organization you might be working for? What's your 'bottom line' for acceptance?	Preparing for the interview	Make sure that the time, place and agenda for the interview are known to the interviewee well before the actual event. Be familiar with the criteria you are selecting for and the job description of the post offered. Read the CV (and note any specific questions that arise from it). Make sure that you are there before the candidate is; it is not clever to keep people waiting; it doesn't make you seem important, it just makes you seem disorganized.
First impressions really do count. Give the interviewer time to settle down before you try and make any complex points. You may have been given a briefing by a recruitment agency, but this may have changed so it is a good idea to confirm the job description early on. It shows that you have done your homework and have taken an interest in the company and makes sure that you are both talking about the same thing. Interviews are two-way. You are choosing them just as much as they are choosing you. It should go without saying, but never tell anything other than the truth at an interview – the potential consequences for you, any agency and your future work prospects are grim. However, you should be positive; don't say 'I've never done that', say 'I have done this, and there are a number of things in common with what you are looking for', then go on to say what they are. You probably have the basic skills required, or you wouldn't be being interviewed.	The interview	Establish rapport with a friendly greeting. Try to sit corner-on to the interviewee rather than facing them across a desk. It is a good idea to start the interview proper by describing the job and how it fits in with the project/company environment. This gives the candidate time to settle down and will rapidly identify any serious mismatches between candidate and the job on offer. When you ask questions try and make them 'open' ones that do not have a yes/no answer. For example, 'In your last contract, what examples can you give me of communicating technical information with non-technical people?', might be a question for someone you were considering to work on a help desk. Listen, listen, listen – and never make any assumptions. Listen with your eyes; the interviewee's body language will tell you as much about what sort of person they are as what they are saying.

Table 7.1 (continued)

Interviewee	Process	Interviewer
It is a good idea to expand on/support any answer you give with examples of real work you have done in the past, it provides the evidence the interviewer needs. Be yourself, don't try and use words you don't ordinarily use, you'll sound false, and don't put on an act, it will be very obvious and can only lose you work. A valuable interviewee skill is that of listening, it is not unknown for the interviewer to have explained what the job is at the start of the interview, spent half an hour with the candidate, and then been asked to describe what the work involves. Refer to questions asked earlier when you can and reflect back the interviewer's own words when appropriate. It helps demonstrate your understanding and builds rapport. These suggestions may seem obvious but lack of attention to them accounts for a large number of interview failures, so you can use them to increase your success rate.	The interview	Don't forget that the interview is two way. Remember that the impression you give the candidate will be the one they take away of both you and the company. The person you interview today could well be tomorrow's customer, or your next interviewer. It is unwise to make a job offer at an interview – you may have other candidates to see, you may need to confer with colleagues/the human resources department, you will certainly need time to think. End the interview on a friendly note but make no promises.

Key points:

- Be punctual
- Be yourself
- Be truthful
- Be positive
- Listen
- First impressions count

Key points:

- Be punctual
- Prepare; read the CV before the interview
- Prepare; have some questions ready
- Let the candidate answer
- Tell the agency and the candidate exactly what the job is
- Define your selection criteria
- Listen with both ears and eyes
- Make no promises

Table 7.1 (continued)

Interviewee	Process	Interviewer
If you are using a recruitment agency let your contact there know how the interview went.	Following up the interview	Now you have to evaluate how the interview went. Did the candidate meet your expectations and criteria?
Then you wait . . .		It is a good idea to write down your impressions immediately after the interview while they are fresh in your mind. It is useful to grade the candidates in some way, perhaps on a scale of 1 (unsuitable) through to 5 (very much above average) against each of the criteria that you prepared before the interview. Be sure to keep records.
If you are applying through an advertisement, and you hear nothing for several days, it is useful to ring the organization and ask if they have any news: if they are going to offer you the job, they will certainly get in touch with you sooner or later, but many organisations do not bother to let you know that you are not being considered at all. A quick call will let you see how the land lies.		
		If you are satisfied with the candidate you will want to offer the job. Before you do this, check with the candidate that he/she is still interested and tell them that you will be following up references.
If the first interview was successful you will either be short-listed, in which case there will be another interview, or you will be offered the job.		Always follow up references. This seems such an obvious step but you would be surprised at how many companies omit this important step – and live to regret it.
If so, now is the time to think about exactly what terms you want and to prepare to negotiate if necessary (see Chapter 9)		

7.3 The appraisal process

A job appraisal interview is one of the major managerial tasks of the leader of a team of people. It is the chance for a team member and his/her manager to look back over the past months and jointly evaluate their performance. The appraisal interview is there to enable you to:

- Plan for the future
- Look at individual performance
- Discuss and plan training and development needs
- Contribute to company career planning, salary planning and job progression
- Evaluate the efficiency of past targets and goals
- Establish priorities for the appraisee and the manager
- Identify, assess and resolve problems
- Look at resourcing needs
- Motivate or re-motivate both the team member and the manager

Job appraisal needs to be systematic if it is to be of any use. All effective managers have day-to-day or week-to-week contact with their team and through this should be aware of what is going on, where the successes and failures are and what 'fire fighting' needs to be done. They will also be running up-dating sessions where they inform their team of corporate, market or local changes in working, policy or law and any changes that affect the workings of their teams. These are the day-to-day tasks of management and quite separate from the annual or biannual appraisal.

The job appraisal interview is an opportunity for the team member and their manager to think about the future months in an organized manner. Before an appraisal they both have the opportunity to think in depth about what they have been doing and where this will lead in the future; where the successes and shortfalls are, and what objectives they will set each other in the future.

7.3.1
The appraisal
process

Table 7.2 The appraisal process from both sides.

The appraisee	Process	The appraiser

Read through your job description and see what has changed, if anything.
 	
Keep careful notes.
 	
Make a list of the goals and targets and standards that you have been set or have set for yourself and rate your success or otherwise in achieving these.
 	
Ask yourself these questions:
 	
● What critical abilities does my job require?
● To what extent do I fulfil them?
● What do I like most about my job?
● What do I like least about my job?
● What, specifically, have I achieved since my last appraisal?
● Were there any goals and standards that I did not meet?
● Could my manager have helped me to do a better job?
● Is there anything my manager does that hinders my performance?
● Is there anything the company does that hinders my performance?
● What changes could be made to improve my performance?
● Does my job make the most of my capabilities?
● How could I become more productive?
● Do I need more experience or training in any aspect of my job?
● How can this be accomplished?
● What have I done since my last appraisal to get ready for more responsibility?
	Before the appraisal	Set a firm date and time for the appraisal and book a quiet room. Allow about two hours for the appraisal interview.
		
		Hold a short meeting with the appraisee to explain the appraisal process and tell him/her what they need to prepare.
		
		Read through the appraisee's job description and see if anything has changed.
		
		Keep careful notes.
		
		Now you will need to review:
		
		● Job requirements to be sure that you really know them
		● Goals and standards you set with the appraisee, plus any notes you have relating to their performance
		● Employee's history, including:
		  – job skills
		  – training
		  – experience
		  – special or unique qualifications
		
		Considering past jobs and past experience:
		
		● Evaluate job performance versus job expectations and rate them from poor to excellent.
		● Note any shortfalls in performance that need to be discussed. Always give specific examples.
		● Consider opportunities or changes for this person. Get ready to give options.

Table 7.2 (continued)

The appraisee	Process	The appraiser
• What new goals and standards should be established for the coming months? • Which old goals and standards need to be changed? • What will I be doing five years from now?	Before the appraisal	
Set your expectations. This is not a contest or an interrogation – it is a planning session for the future.	The interview	Set your expectations; this is as much about your performance as a manager as it is about the performance of the appraisee.
Bring all the notes you have made and be punctual.		Gather all your notes and start on time.
Create rapport with your appraiser by having a friendly attitude and relaxed body language.		Make sure that there will be no interruptions and that the room is comfortable. A cup of tea or coffee will relax the appraisee.
Try to follow the agenda.		Set an agenda for the appraisal. A sample agenda might contain the following: • General overview on progress so far • Measurement of specific goals and targets • Areas of concern • New goals and targets for the coming year and the measurements associated with these • Development plans Work towards a positive close to the meeting. As far as possible follow the pattern of appraisee to speak first, then appraiser to comment
These are the communication skills that you will need to use during the appraisal: • Make no assumptions about what the appraiser is thinking or feeling • Listen actively and encouragingly • Be as specific as possible • Don't avoid difficult subjects • Use positive words as far as possible • Don't be afraid to ask for help • Keep notes		These are the communication skills that you will need to use during the appraisal: • Make no assumptions about what the appraisee is thinking or feeling • Listen actively and encourage the appraisee to speak • Be as specific as possible • Don't avoid difficult subjects • Summarize from time to time • Keep notes

Table 7.2 (continued)

The appraisee	Process	The appraiser
Read your appraisal form carefully and sign it if you agree it represents what was said and decided. If you are unclear about anything or don't agree with what it says, sort this out as soon as possible. Keep your copy of the appraisal form – it is your 'route map' for the coming year.	Following up the appraisal	Fill in the appraisal form (if you have one) and then pass it on to the appraisee for it to read and sign that they agree with what it says. If there are any areas that are unclear or that the appraisee does not agree with, you need to sort these out as soon as possible. File your copy of the appraisal form.

7.4 Summary

The communications skills associated with interviews and appraisals are very important ones. At the very least they can make the difference between being employed and unemployed. However, these skills are also extremely important in the longer term. When you are recruiting it is essential that you make the right decision; if it is your own business your livelihood may depend on it!

Similarly, applying good communication practices to the appraisal process will ensure that career progression has the best chance of success from the point of view of both parties. This chapter has covered the communications aspects of both sides of interviews and appraisals and has shown how they relate back to the basics of communications as described in Chapter 2.

7.5 Exercises

Why is it important to make sure that both parties to an interview or appraisal are communicating effectively? Why are assumptions a threat to this?

What are the key points for an interviewer and an interviewee? Give examples from your own, or colleagues' experience that illustrate where failure to observe some, or all of these points has caused problems.

7.5.1 Role play

With two people, one taking the role of interviewer and the other of interviewee, run an interview for the following situation. The job is to be a junior reporter for a local newspaper. The candidate has the relevant qualifications but has not worked for three months, but has been actively involved in charity work during this period. The interviewer is the assistant editor and is looking for someone with good local contacts, not necessarily any previous professional journalistic experience, and someone able to express themselves in an entertaining and effective way. If this is to be a group exercise then other members of the group should take notes and be prepared to make comments on how it might be handled better. Consider producing dummy job adverts, CVs and job specifications to expand the exercise.

7.5.2
Role play

The successful candidate has been with the newspaper for a year and has done very well with getting around to local events and getting the information but has needed rather more editorial assistance in writing articles than had been expected. Set up an appraisal interview in the same way as for the interview with the goal of setting the matter right by agreeing on a training course and an action plan to reduce the editorial assistance needed over a period of time. This could be expanded into a series of appraisals that chart five years' progress from junior reporter to assistant editor.

8   Negotiation

'Looking at bargains from a purely commercial point of view, someone is always cheated, but looked at with the simple eye both seller and buyer always win.' Vid Grayson, 1907.

8.1 Introduction

Negotiate: To confer (with another) for the purpose of arranging some matter by mutual *agreement.* (Shorter Oxford Dictionary)

A key element in all business communications is negotiation. Some people are natural negotiators and others have it thrust upon them, but it is a fact of life that everything is negotiable. However, negotiation is not a black art. The principles of the negotiation process have been well established. This chapter describes what may be negotiated, strategies that can be employed to meet different negotiation situations, and the cycle of negotiation. The concepts are presented in a two-part case study that is based on a real situation.

8.2 Negotiate a better deal

8.2.1 Introduction: establishing what can be negotiated

Ask freelance workers what there is to negotiate in a contract and most will say, 'the hourly rate'. The more sophisticated might also mention the start date and agreed time off for a pre-booked holiday, but that is really only the beginning. We've come up with over 25 points that you could negotiate in a typical freelance deal. Figure 8.1 shows them in the form of a 'mind-map'; this starts from the concept of a deal and goes down different paths based on the major components of fees, conditions of work and contract terms. Some of the individual points are then elaborated on to give an idea of what to look for.

8.2.2 Negotiables

Fees

This isn't just the hourly or daily rate! There are all sorts of other factors that can result in money in the bank. For example, many agencies and some companies will give you a fee for introducing new staff to a site, and within reason you can always negotiate the agency's own margin (you don't want them to go out of business, so don't be greedy) particularly for follow-on assignments. There is also the possibility of negotiating a fixed-price deal for certain well-defined jobs (if you're feeling brave and know what you're doing). You should also consider if you want to be paid hourly/daily or even weekly, particularly when the option of working at home presents itself; you can often do a week's work in less than a week and this is a significant benefit.

Rate

Even the rate is open to interpretation; it isn't just pounds per hour/day. You can also look at such things as overtime rates for long hours or weekend working, which can make a significant difference to what you actually earn. Operational jobs might involve being on call or

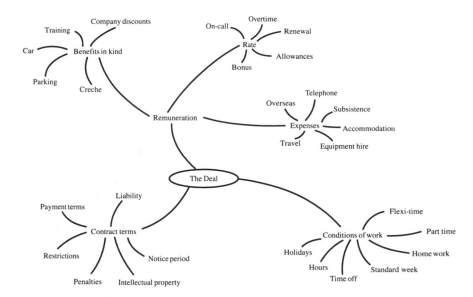

Figure 8.1 Mind-map of negotiating a deal

working shifts, again a significant source of extra income. Then there are the possibilities of agreed increases on renewal or bonuses for finishing work early.

Benefits in kind

Although not likely to have an effect on the fatness of your wallet, benefits in kind can be a significant plus when negotiating your deal. They don't cost the other side anything like as much as cash and can be effectively tax free (not always though, so get advice). For example you might be able to get training, even if it is out of normal working hours, or you may be given access to company discount schemes.

Expenses

These can make a dramatic difference to your earnings, particularly for those working abroad. For example, if you are paid for a return flight to the UK each week and only go home every other week the cash soon mounts up, even at bucket-shop prices. In certain circumstances such expenses can be largely tax free. There may also be incidental expenses such as subsistence when you have to visit other company sites. Where the client allows you to work based at home, say two days a week on site, three at home, you may be able to claim the cost of your travel to and from the client's site and related expenses.

Contract terms

Very few people think about this when they consider a new assignment or job. This is a pity because, apart from it always being a good idea to read a contract before you sign it, there are a number of negotiables to be found here. The most obvious one is the payment period. A few years ago almost all temporary agencies paid weekly, then in the recession monthly payments became the norm, as the cash flow just wasn't there. However, it is well worth haggling over this as many agencies will at least consider better terms, particularly if it makes the difference between winning the business and not.

The notice period should also be considered, particularly where the terms are unequal, such as you must give a month's notice and they need only give a week. There is also the possibility of penalty and liability clauses which you should make sure you're happy with, and if you need additional insurance this will cost money. Another point might be limitations on your working for other companies which are customers of the agency without going through them. Similarly you may find yourself prohibited from working for the client except through the agency for a six- or twelve-month period. While such clauses are common to protect the agency's investment, some agencies put in excessive limitations which, if enforced, could make life difficult for you if you fell out with them. The final point to consider here concerns intellectual property. If you do any work outside of that for the client, for example magazine articles, you must make sure that the contract is worded to allow you to do so. Or you might find that the book you slaved away writing at weekends belongs to the agency or the client not you!

Conditions of work

This concerns the restrictions that apply to you when delivering the goods. What hours do you have to work? For example can you work 8 till 4 instead of 9 till 5 if it makes your travelling easier? Another possibility that is getting easier to sell is that of working from home, assuming you have a suitable working environment there. This is a major benefit as it cuts down significantly on travel costs and also gives you an extra couple of hours in the day to yourself. Not to mention the ability to fit the hours to your own requirements (particularly useful to people with young children, time-consuming hobbies, or magazine articles to write). You might also wish to agree specific breaks in the contract to cover pre-booked holidays or other special events. Where overtime is not available you may be able to agree a time off in lieu arrangement instead.

To show that this is not all theoretical I offer the following example from personal experience in negotiating a contract. The rate on offer was less than I usually get, though only marginally and it was based further away than I consider a comfortable drive, and I don't work away from my home base unless I'm actually threatened with starvation; there was also a point about not doing any other work for the duration of the contract. A little research established that I could get there conveniently by British Rail, and to my surprise the travelling has worked out well! It was also agreed at the interview that working at home when practical was an option. This left the issue of the rate and the work restriction to be dealt with. The agency started by saying that fees would be paid monthly, I suggested weekly was more like it and we settled on fortnightly. This improved cash flow arrangement made up for the marginally lower rate so that sorted that out. The work restriction was dealt with by the insertion of a clause in the contract to the effect that I could write magazine articles and the like provided there was no conflict of interest with the client and that I was able to deliver the hours requested. There were a couple of other small points arising from the contract which were also sorted out easily but I think you get the general idea. Admittedly this involved me in more work than just saying 'yes' to the original deal and it certainly made the agent earn the commission, but in the end everyone got what they wanted.

This type of negotiation is often referred to as 'changing the package'. The overall value of the deal remains much the same. It is the components included that change.

**8.2.3
Summary**

When you next come to negotiate something, first define what it is you actually want, not only in terms of price, but considering other points. This may not make you flavour of the day with the other party to the negotiation, but it should end up with everyone getting a better deal.

Discussion

What negotiable factors exist when buying a window-cleaning business? And for selling a hifi and electrical goods store? What are the common elements to both negotiations?

**8.3
Negotiate a better deal using negotiation strategies**

8.3.1
Negotiation strategies

Figure 8.2 Mind-map of negotiation strategies

The first thing to do is choose the strategy you are going to use. There are five main approaches that you should consider: win/lose, put it off, look at both sides, co-operate, and solve the problem.

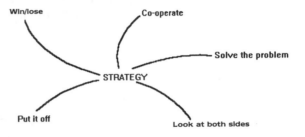

Win/lose

This is the adversarial approach, in that you are negotiating to get the best deal you possibly can at the expense of the other party. While this can be a successful one-off strategy it does not work in the long term with people whom you intend to deal with twice. You should only consider this when dealing with absolute non-negotiables or when you don't want to work with the same supplier or client again.

Put it off

In this case you are simply putting off the negotiation to another day. In general this does not help you, as you will still need to deal eventually or the contract may have gone away to someone else. However, it may be useful if you want to buy a little time while waiting on the outcome of another interview or the result of further research. Be sure to identify how long you can put off the decision without losing out altogether.

Look at both sides

The essence of this is to make a conscious effort to listen to both sides of the deal and summarize the key points to ensure understanding. It is an essential part of any good negotiation strategy and is useful at any point in a negotiation.

Co-operate

In this strategy each party recognizes the other's positions and respects that viewpoint. This is an excellent starting point for any negotiation and is a recommended strategy to adopt.

Solve the problem

In this approach you work with another party to define a joint solution to the problem, i.e. to agree a contract. The result of such a strategy should be a 'win/win' deal which will lay firm foundations for future trading. However, to do this requires a certain amount of preparation where you and the other party get together to discuss all the points, and time constraints may prevent its adoption in complex deals. It also requires that others involved wish to adopt a similar strategy and this is not always certain. This works well where the sale is complicated because of unusual customer requirements and where working within a team or consortium has enabled the deal to be closed.

The benefits of 'co-operate and look at both sides' is that they should enable you to get a first-rate deal and protect your long-term interests. You may find it useful to consider using the 'put it off' strategy from time to time and the 'co-operate' strategy could be useful for difficult sales. However, use win/lose at your peril.

Discussion

Discuss what might be the best strategy to use in the following situations: selling a magazine article to a local newspaper; asking for an increase in pay; buying a holiday at the last minute; renegotiating a deadline for a magazine article?

8.3.2
The negotiation cycle

Once you have decided on the strategy you can then get going on the actual negotiation. There is a simple five-step life cycle that can be applied to negotiation: plan, explore, offer, barter, close, as shown in Figure 8.3.

Figure 8.3 The negotiation cycle

Plan

You need to identify what it is you want and then prioritize it into high, medium and low priorities. The high-priority items are the things that you really must have, such as an absolute minimum hourly rate, a maximum commuting distance, minimum duration of employment. This is your bottom line. The medium-priority items are those that you would prefer to have but can survive without, for example flexible working hours, use of a creche and at least six months work. The low-priority items are those which you might like but are certainly not worth risking losing the deal for. Examples include access to company sports facilities, use of subsidized staff restaurant, parking space.

At this stage you should also establish with whom you are negotiating. In the case of temporary staff this is complicated by the fact that there may be an intermediary between you and the client. You may be negotiating with a job agency as well as the company for whom you'll be working, so you should try and define which parts of the deal affect which parties most. Typically the agency is concerned with its margin and cash flow more than anything else. The customer is also concerned with rate but is the one with whom you would negotiate conditions of work, expenses, and benefits in kind etc. Similar situations can occur when you are trying to sell something to a company. You may be dealing with the people who wish to use the equipment but you have to get the order from a central purchasing department. The role of the people you negotiate with will have an effect on how they negotiate. This brings us to the concept of decision makers and influencers.

Decision makers are the people who actually make the decision to buy or not, who put their name on the contract or cheque.

Influencers are those involved in making the decision but who do not take the final responsibility for it. Typically they are advisors, technical specialists, legal experts.

It is important to establish that the person you are dealing with is the person that makes the decisions. For example, you may be dealing with an employee at your local bank while negotiating an overdraft or loan. However, decisions as to the rate of interest and maximum loan you can have may be taken at a regional level. In this case you will be dealing with the local bank employee as your intermediary, who will have the role of an influencer but not a decision maker.

Discussion

How would you deal differently with decision makers and influencers? Have you any recent examples where you have come across influencers? How did you deal with them?

Explore

It is easy to miss this stage out and jump straight into the negotiations from the word go. However, this is a mistake, as you can miss vital information, and by failing to establish rapport with the other person can risk misunderstanding their meaning.

When trying to gain information you should use open questions – asking questions for which there is no yes/no answer – which encourages the person to talk more freely and so tell you what they think. You should always summarize what you have understood and gain agreement so that you are sure you are both negotiating about the same thing.

Offer

This is where the negotiation begins in earnest. Both parties will make their starting position clear. Yours might be £27 per hour, paid weekly, flexible working hours and a rate review after three months; theirs might be £25 per hour, monthly payments, fixed for six months. It is important that you leave yourself room to manoeuvre, if your bottom line was £25 then you should have not made it your opening bid. Similarly you don't want to show all your bargaining counters up front, you need to keep them in reserve so you can make additional offers. You can introduce them using the 'if . . . then . . .' technique where you make acceptance of one point conditional upon accepting another.

Barter

This is the real nitty-gritty part of the negotiation and how you handle matters here will profoundly affect the outcome of the process. A key point is never to give anything away without getting something back in return. For example, the client may say that they can only pay £24 per hour when you were asking for £25. Don't just say 'yes', say 'yes, but I want a review after three months'. Whenever you are bargaining make any changes conditional – 'If you . . .then I . . .'. For example, 'If you want me to work excess hours without a special overtime rate then I want to be able to take time off in lieu'. A useful ploy is to link issues when bargaining. You can then play off one factor against another. Typically you might link a requirement for working long hours to meet deadlines with the ability to work at home.

As this can start to get complicated, even with a simple supply contract, you should take notes as you go along so that you know where you are. And never forget the bottom line that you identified up-front; never go below this.

Close

This is the end of the process. You have agreed a deal and defined what the terms are going to be. It is vitally important that both parties think they have agreed to the same deal so it is essential that you not only write it down yourself but go over it again with the other person to make sure that they have the same understanding that you do. While you are doing this you should reinforce the benefits that you are both getting from the deal and be prepared to be firm, should it seem that negotiations are about to open up again.

8.4 Summary

What at first sight may seem to be a simple black and white situation when it comes down to serious negotiation is often a multi-faceted, many-coloured affair. Money is not the only negotiable and 'changing the package' is a key element in negotiation. It is necessary to analyze all aspects of the deal before starting any negotiation and to determine what your real 'bottom line' is on all the factors involved. Furthermore, there are different strategies that are appropriate for different types of negotiation depending on who you are dealing with and what you wish to achieve. In addition the concept of the negotiation cycle has been introduced showing the time element and how it can affect the dynamics of a negotiation.

8.5
Exercises

8.5.1
Open questions

Here is a list of 'closed questions' where you could reasonably expect an answer of 'yes' or 'no'. This sort of question is not helpful in a negotiation since a blunt answer does not move the negotiation forward. Rephrase the questions in a way that will both gain more information from the person you are negotiating with and open up new avenues for negotiation.

1 'Are you prepared to sell this car for £6,000?'
2 'Can I have delivery of the washing machine by next Thursday?'
3 'So you are only offering two weeks holiday that must be taken in July?'
4 'Is there a policy for career planning in your company?'
5 'If I order 10 you'll charge me £6 each?'
6 'So you want to pay over the next two years?'

8.5.2
Planning a negotiation

Before you negotiate it is essential to plan just what it is you are prepared to accept, not accept or compromise about. It is very helpful to draw up a systematic priority list. In this exercise you are about to buy a new or slightly used car from a motor dealer. You will be using this car for business as well as pleasure. You have never met the dealer before. You have a fixed amount to spend and cannot go over budget.

Best case: worst case

Using your own preferences, make a 'best case: worst case' list. These are the things that concern you to a greater or lesser degree:

Price, warranty, mileage, cost of spare parts, fuel consumption, colour, metallic paint, styling, interior trim, radio, CD player, mobile phone, insurance, top speed, security, safety features, engine capacity, payment method, delivery, motor club membership, breakdown service, road tax, baby seats, resale value, free car if your car is being repaired, reliability, availability of spare parts, size of car, boot space, sun roof, electric windows, first-aid kit, air bags, alloy wheel-trim, retractable aerial, dimensions, servicing, cost of respraying, customized numberplate.

Research

What else should you research before you begin the negotiation?

8.5.3
The outcome of the negotiation

Often a negotiation is not only about a fair price for goods or services or a fair rate of pay, or even about working conditions; it may also involve working relationships and the interaction between yourself and the other negotiator after the negotiation is completed. The result of the negotiation may even set a precedent that would be difficult to change in the future. This exercise looks at not only the negotiation itself but at the outcomes of the negotiation and the necessity to make the solution work.

You are the very organized and efficient secretary to the Marketing Manager of a large company. Over the next three weeks your manager has asked you to work late and although there will be overtime pay for the extra hours you will work you have a problem: you have just moved house and desperately need to get things straight, also you were going to ask for two mornings off in the near future to deal with the gas and electricity suppliers. You also have three unbreakable evening engagements in the next two weeks. You know that a great deal of the extra work is not complicated and could easily be done by a temp or one of the office juniors (it would not be difficult to arrange this). You like your boss and know that she is basically very fair but she is an enthusiast and easily gets carried away when she is interested in what she is doing. Indeed, she is fascinated by the new reports that she has to prepare over the next three weeks and you know that she is likely to be quite happy working very long hours, possibly feeling that she needs you at her side. One additional piece of information is that there is an expensive training course coming up in two months that you would very much like to attend.

Preparation

How would you prepare for your negotiation?

Solution

What will you need to do to make the solution work?

9 Conflict handling

'Arguments are to be avoided; they are always vulgar and often convincing.' Oscar Wilde

9.1 Introduction

Life is difficult, but, like growing old, it is significantly better than the alternative. In particular working life can be fraught with difficulties, coming in many forms but usually caused by your colleagues. There is no way to avoid these troubles but there are things you can do to make them easier to deal with. This chapter on conflict handling will show how you can use communication skills to make dealing with difficult situations easier. It also shows how poor communication is often at the root of many conflicts.

9.2 Causes

What are the main causes of difficult situations? Practical research has shown that there are five main causes of conflicts:

- Assumptions – you can't be sure that everyone has the same ones until they're tested.
- Communication – when this is poor you can be working with incomplete information.
- Priority – where individuals have different priorities regarding people and tasks.
- Speed – where people have different speeds and ways of working.
- Status/territory – this concerns space, money, power, even a desire to keep secrets.

9.2.1 Assumptions

Harry knows that the deadline for the report has been brought forward a week. Jane does not know this, she has not been told, and thinks there is plenty of time to complete the job. The following exchange occurred:

Harry: 'Why are you off out to lunch? We've only got two days left!'
Jane: 'What's that got to do with you? I don't need your permission to have lunch, and what do you mean there are two days left!'

You must always ensure that everyone involved in a meeting or conversation is working from the same knowledge base, particularly if there are time/workload pressures involved. To do otherwise is to risk conflicts that arise from making false assumptions.

9.2.2 Communication

A simple instruction passed on without checking understanding can lead to all sorts of problems later on. In this example Henrietta thought she was to meet with Janet at 10:30 outside the head-office reception. In fact she was supposed to meet her inside reception (in fact she was told 'at') and they spent half an hour waiting within ten feet of each other before Janet went into reception to make a call to find out where Henrietta was. The conversation went something like this:

Janet   seeing Henrietta arrive (or so she thought):
'Where on earth have you been? I've been waiting for ages! I've got better things to do than wait all day for you to get your act together, even if you haven't.'

Henrietta You've got a nerve, you've been waiting in the wrong place, and it's freezing out there.'

9.2.3
Priority

Your priorities are not necessarily those of the other people involved in a project or piece of work. Consider the following situation. You wish to arrange a meeting to discuss a problem with a client. You consider this to be important because you think the order may be lost; £2,000 of business and your related commission is at stake. You want this meeting now! Your partner, who is the only one who can resolve the problem, is working on a campaign to win £10,000-worth of new business. To her it is more important to win the new business than lose the old business. You have different priorities and this could lead to a conflict.

9.2.4
Speed

People have different ways of working. This can make itself shown in many different ways – speed, amount of information they need, what motivates them etc. However, of these factors the one that tends to be the most likely to lead to conflict is speed. This does not refer to how hard people work, or even how quickly they can perform a particular task. It refers to the speed with which they reach a decision or accept a change. For instance, two people both have access to the same information and have the same long-term goals. They have been given a project to do together within a fixed time frame. One person may be a real speed merchant and want to get something done right away, the other may want time to reflect on all the factors involved, dotting every I and crossing every T. Working together they may find that arguments arise along the lines of, 'We really need to get going on this. Let's order the parts' met with, 'Hang on a minute. I'm not quite sure that we should. We may be risking ordering some of the wrong parts. Let's think about it a bit more.'

9.2.5
Status and territory

This is one of the simplest to understand. Human beings are territorial by nature – even very small children have a strong sense of what is their territory. This is not just physical items such as your desk, your computer, your locker, it is also intellectual and social. People consider their ideas and their colleagues as belonging to their territory as well. So it is not surprising that when someone's/some group's territory is trespassed on without due consideration and consultation that conflicts arise.

Discussion

What conflicts have you experienced or observed in the last two weeks? What do you think was the cause of these conflicts? Do the causes map onto the generic causes given above?

**9.3
Common situations**

The most common difficult situations in the work place are being 'dumped on' and being criticised. Both these situations are covered in what is known as 'assertiveness training'. In recent years there have been a lot of assertiveness training courses for women, and some men think that this is just a way of women learning to become more aggressive to compete with them. Nothing could be further from the truth – these courses teach the difference between assertion and aggression and how to utilize the former to reduce conflict and increase your options, for both men and women.

**9.3.1
Assertion versus
aggression**

Aggression is based upon contempt for others; people who act this way are relying on others to cave in. Assertiveness is based upon respect for both yourself and for those with whom you deal. Successful assertive behaviour includes being able clearly to communicate what you feel and being able to say what you want while taking into account how this will affect others.

Discussion

Give examples of aggressive behaviour that you have seen during the last month. How might the situation have been diffused? Discuss how you might be more assertive in your day-to-day life and how it might improve matters for all involved.

**9.3.2
How to say 'no'**

This is one of the basic building blocks of assertion. Many people in business find it very hard indeed to say no, for many reasons:

● They may feel that they have no right to say no.
● They may like the feeling of responsibility and usefulness that doing things for others brings.
● They may feel that they must always say yes to their managers.
● They may feel that saying no will damage the relationship between themselves and the person making the demand of them.
● They may not even know what is expected of them as part of the tasks and duties that their job entails.

In fact, the ability to say no is one of the primary business skills. Just think what could happen if we always said yes:

● We would find it hard to get our essential tasks done because we would be forever accommodating others.
● We would be overburdened with extra work.
● Job descriptions would be meaningless.
● Timetables would be meaningless.
● Standards and procedures could be altered at whim.

The essence of dealing with being dumped on is covered by showing people how to say 'no'. People often make unreasonable demands on their fellow workers whether they be peers or subordinates. Saying no to unreasonable demands is not something that everyone feels comfortable with. Most people know someone who drowns in work because they just take what is given, even when they can see that the rest of their team is having a really lazy time. Two points should be borne in mind – you don't need to apologize when you say 'no', and you don't need to explain why except where it is professionally necessary to do so. That said you should always be positive about any explanation that you do give.

For example, 'No, I'm not going to repair that video recorder. It isn't a machine I've ever used and it would be impossible for me to learn it in the time available for the job. However, I believe the Manchester office has someone with the relevant skills and I'd be happy to find out the details for you.' You state your position clearly and positively and show yourself in as good a light as possible.

There are several ways of saying no assertively:

- Say no and do not explain. Use a pleasant tone of voice but be firm.
- Say no and then explain your reasons. Again use a pleasant tone of voice, but be firm.
- Say no, explain why you have done so and then provide an alternative solution. Remember the pleasant tone of voice and the firmness.

Here are some examples:

'Would you take these letters to the post?'
'No, I must finish this report.'

'The photocopier has broken down again, come and show me how to fix it.'
'No, I don't know anything about that photocopier.'

'Will you re-organize the filing cabinet this afternoon?'
'No, I'm on a training course this afternoon. But I'm free tomorrow lunchtime and I can do it then.'

Discussion

Work out different ways in which you can say no without seeming negative. How might you apply this to domestic situations, such as not doing the washing up, this time, because you want to go out?

9.3.3
Handling criticism

Handling criticism comes in two flavours, dealing with valid criticism, and dealing with invalid criticism. Accepting valid criticism assertively means accepting the criticism by repeating it back to the critic, showing that you understand it, offering any necessary apology (be brief) and finishing with a positive statement on the way forward. For example you may be told that 'You've set the project back a month because you didn't read the program spec. and did your own thing.' Assuming this is the case a good response might go along the lines of, 'I didn't read the spec. and I accept that I should have done, but I thought I understood what was wanted. I realize this was a mistake and I'm sorry, but I have learnt from this and it is going to make me more productive in the future.'

If you accept valid criticism calmly and look for a positive course of action then the whole situation is likely to remain serene and you will gain the reputation of being positive, a good one to have. However, invalid criticism should not be accepted. As with valid criticism you should show that you understand what is being said by repeating it back to your critic while saying that you don't agree with it. For example ' No, I did not forget to back up the system disk last night, I have the tape here.' You should keep your voice firm when refuting invalid criticism and make sure your general demeanour is consistent with what you are saying. If what is said makes you angry or upset and you choose to let this be known, do this with a statement about yourself, not about the critic, such as, say 'I am angry that you imply I am not doing my job properly' rather than 'You've upset me'. The goal is to refute the criticism without raising the overall level of tension. The old-fashioned advice of count to ten before you reply is a good one if you aren't sure about your own temper.

Discussion

Thinking about how you have criticised/been criticised in the last week, how was that presented and how did you, or the person criticised, respond? What would have made the criticism more effective for both parties?

9.4
Good conflict handling

The essence of good conflict handling is: take a step back to find the facts; look at the situation from as many angles as possible; ask people to explain what they think should happen; look for the best possible situation all-round; and sell its benefits to all concerned.

When conflict arises we have an array of possible strategies for handling it. These can be divided into three types:

Aggressive conflict handling
I win/you lose
Dismiss the opposition

Passive conflict handling
Put it off
Compromise

Assertive conflict handling
Look at both sides
Find a solution

9.4.1
Aggressive strategies

These strategies use no negotiation. They are not concerned with any possible rightness or justice, simply with winning the conflict. These strategies invariably result in a win/lose situation which may be all very well for the victor, but not good for the vanquished. Conflicts that are managed in this way are not really resolved – they usually recur later when the vanquished has regrouped and restored his/her strength and has the (probably quite legitimate) feeling that he/she is 'owed one'.

Obviously there are times in business when there can be no negotiation, for instance over things like safety procedures, legal procedures or some disciplinary matters. However, the attitude 'I will win at all costs' is not the most effective one. It is far better to use an assertive strategy instead. In the case of a business negotiation – for instance over the cost of a product or service – the I win/you lose strategy is short-term; it is not really worth gaining an individual sale if you eventually lose a customer.

9.4.2
Passive strategies

These strategies result in a lose/lose situation, where neither party gets the result they wanted. The conflict is never really resolved and will recur later. There is however some merit in the 'put it off' strategy when tempers are running high and a period of 'cooling off ' would make the next stage of the conflict management easier.

9.4.3
Assertive strategies

These are the most successful strategies, resulting in a win/win situation and a true resolution of the conflict. Be prepared to spend extra time when using these strategies since they involve a thorough investigation of both sides of the argument and careful planning of the outcome of the conflict.

9.4.4
Action plan for constructive, assertive conflict management

Define the problem

Firstly you need a clear statement of what is going wrong, what has caused the conflict and how each person feels about this. Until the problem has been carefully defined, neither party can be certain of what is actually happening. There is a natural tendency in all of us to see our side of things clearly and pay much less attention to other's viewpoints.

At this point each person involved in the conflict should clearly state what has been happening. An effort must be made to hear the other person out calmly and there should be no interruptions.

Rules

● No interrupting.
● Talk about what has actually occurred, not what you think should have happened.
● No personal attacks or 'name calling'.
● Calmly ask for clarification if any of the points made are unclear.
● No general statements – be as precise as possible.
● All sides must put their case.
● Summarize at the end of each statement.

Analyse the causes

What caused the problem? Again, all sides must contribute. A genuine attempt to understand why the problem or conflict has arisen and a genuine desire to resolve the conflict must be present.

Rules

● No interrupting.
● Try to keep to the subject – extraneous matter should not be dragged in.
● Try not to use 'blaming' language. You are not looking at whose fault it is, just at what started the conflict.
● All sides must put their case.
● Summarize at the end of each statement.

Look for a solution

Each party should try to define what they would like as an outcome of the conflict. This should not be a listing of reparations or demands, but a careful statement of what they would like to occur in terms of actions.

Rules

- No interrupting.
- Look for positive outcomes.
- Any solutions should be reasonable and must look at what limits and restrictions exist.
- Try to be creative.

Select a solution

Most conflicts within the business area are solvable – we are not talking about hostage taking or the Third World War. A reasonable solution is always possible if both parties genuinely want the conflict to cease. It is probable that most of the demands made at the height of the conflict were exaggerated or simply a bargaining position that would be adjusted later. By now, if the first three stages have been covered, it will be much easier for the parties to talk more reasonably and see that a positive outcome is possible. It is at this stage that the 'trade off' principle comes into force: 'If you do such and such, then I'll do this and that' is a good starting point.

Rules

- Keep the idea that a solution is possible to the forefront.
- You are not making concessions – you are trying to solve the problem.
- Think of the consequences if the conflict is not resolved.
- Be fair.

Implement the solution

Make an action plan. What will need to be done to stop the conflict reoccurring? Make a real commitment to communicate throughout the resolution of the conflict. Feedback is essential, just because you have decided what you are going to do does not mean that each person involved believes that this will happen. If the conflict was a severe one and the solution is complicated it may be necessary to put in some controls such as deadlines for remedial action or procedures that will ensure that changes really take place.

Rules

- No 'dragging the body about' or recriminations.
- Be positive.
- Use realistic time scales.
- Keep a record of what you have agreed to do.
- Both sides must agree.

9.4.5
Conclusion

The win/win approach to interactions was much publicized in the 1960s in books such as *Games People Play* (1968) Enc Beme, Penguin and *I'm OK, You're OK* (1967), Thomas Harris, New York Grove Press which cover transactional analysis. The basic idea is that a good transaction is one where both parties win. For example, you may wish to take a holiday but the project is near a critical stage. The bald statement 'I'm away at the end of the month for a week, just thought you'd like to know' is not going to go down well and could well be the end of the contract. An alternative would be to say 'I'd like to go away for a week but I realize that we've got a milestone coming up, so I've agreed with Chandra that she will cover for me that week and I can work some extra hours next week to deal with the critical code needed to finish off my module. What do you think?' This provides the basis for negotiation and indicates not only an understanding of other's problems but a willingness to solve them. It is much harder for someone to say 'no' if you take this sort of approach.

Discussion

Discuss how you might apply win/win approaches to handling conflicts. Why is such an approach preferable to one which might result in a one-off win?

At the risk of taking a more philosophical approach, the following checklist, taken from *Constructive Conflict Management: Managing To Make a Difference* by John Crawley, Nicholas Brealey Publishing Ltd, London, 1995, is offered for consideration. This defines the beliefs that are likely to produce a successful outcome to a conflict.

- It is possible to solve problems. We can handle the complexities of life.
- I don't need to argue to be powerful.
- Be willing to let go.
- Many things do work.
- Expect a lot of yourself and others.
- Much human suffering can be eliminated.
- There is no such thing as a stupid question.
- There is very little which is none of your/my business.
- There are other ways.
- You can get somewhere with anyone.
- It is possible for everyone to win.
- It is possible to trust ourselves and others.

9.5 Summary

Dealing with behaviour and situations you find difficult is largely a case of using that rare commodity, common sense. Keeping your cool, identifying what the real problems are and acting positively and constructively will get you a long way. Learning the difference between assertion and aggression and making sure you put that learning into practice will also help. Finally, always keep in mind that the solution to any conflict does exist, you only have to find it.

9.6 Exercises

9.6.1 Saying 'no'

You have been asked to go to the bank by your manager. This is not part of your job description and it will take you at least half an hour to do this and you have a deadline to meet. Think of as many constructive ways of saying 'no' to this request as you can.

9.6.2 Aggression versus assertion

What is the difference between aggression and assertion? Illustrate this with examples of each type of behaviour in a workplace setting.

9.6.3
Handling a conflict

Two people, who are only in the office part of the time, have to share a desk. What conflicts are likely to arise and how would you go about stopping them?

9.6.4
Causes of conflicts

What are the main causes of conflicts? Give examples from your own experience of conflicts that have been generated by these causes.

9.6.5
Wrong assumptions

Give an example where you have had a disagreement with someone based on an assumption that you, or the other person had made. How might you prevent conflicts that are based upon wrong assumptions?

10 Time management

'Oh my ears and whiskers, how late it's getting!' The White Rabbit, *Alice in Wonderland*

10.1 Introduction

Time management is the key to organizing many of the activities that are required to communicate effectively. This chapter provides the basic skills needed to make sure you have time to get your message across well. The essential elements of time management are provided together with exercises that will allow them to be implemented in both working and social life. If you can't manage your time effectively you will not have the time to communicate effectively either.

In the 1980s time management became a growth market – specialist diaries designed to help people use their time more efficiently were a boom industry. In those days there were even people who had two or three of these things, one for work, one for leisure and one for luck! There were people who said that 'It has changed my life', a sort of religious conversion apparently. However, in some cases that was actually true. It had changed the person's life. They had gone from being disorganized and late for almost every meeting to actually showing every sign of being efficient. Managing your time effectively will give you significant benefits in both working and social spheres of activity and can result in a much improved quality of life.

10.2 What is it?

What is time management and how do you learn it? Partly it is being organized about what you do but, more importantly, it is organizing things to fit with the way you live and work. Like everything else you can be taught it, but it is actually quite simple to do for yourself. Many people do it naturally and just call it common sense which, as everyone knows, is a rare commodity.

Time management: Managing your time so that it is apportioned to what is most important to you and your business.

10.3
Key elements

The key elements of time management are: planning; prioritizing; performing; filing; and delegation.

10.3.1
Planning

Many people are very good at this, they do it by making lists, and essentially that is all there is to planning. A simple hardback A4 notebook covers all the requirements for planning. Expensive diaries are optional. You should take time at the beginning of each month, week and day to list the following things:

Table 10.1

Business tasks	Such as:
	meetings
	planning activities
	financial activities
	selling activities
	reporting activities
	appointments
	conferences
Housekeeping tasks	Such as:
	filing
	briefing staff
	being briefed
	promised actions (by you/others)
	thinking time
	research time
	delegation
	personal appointments
	checking activities
	handling the post
	shopping
	telephoning
Fixed tasks/activities	Such as:
	travelling
	lunch
	breaks
	holidays
	birthdays/anniversaries/congratulations

Note that the list must include not just work-related items but time and tasks for your personal life as well. Time management will not help you if you attempt to apply it to only part of your life. That doesn't mean that you have to plan your weekends and evenings in the same way that you do your working time, or with the same priorities, but you must make sure that if you need to be at a restaurant by 19:30 on Tuesday you have made sure that you have planned for it so that no-one is going to expect you to work late on that day.

10.3.2
Prioritizing

You've got your list of what is to be done and that is half the battle. The next most important thing is to prioritize how you're going to deal with the items on the list. If you fail to do this you can easily end up hopelessly switching from task to task and never actually doing anything, a bit like a kitten chasing its tail. There are four attributes to identify for each task in the list: importance; imminence; fixed/movable, high/low return on effort.

Importance

Do other activities depend on getting this task done? (tidying up your filing system, buying stationery for the office, ordering spare parts for the repair shop etc.) Do other people's tasks depend on your getting this task done? (for example, setting tasks for your staff, getting correspondence to the postroom, etc.) Does the value of this task outweigh the value of other tasks? (for example, Is conducting an appraisal review more important than tidying up your office? Is seeing a customer more important than filling in your expenses sheet?)

Imminence

Must this task be done by a particular time – is there a deadline set (for example, today, later in the week)?

Fixed/movable

Is this task fixed to a set timescale (for example, meetings, end of the month reports)? Or can it be moved (for example, having a drink after work with a colleague)?

High/low return on effort

How much will the effort you expend in doing this task repay you in terms of profit, time saved, smooth running of business? For example, would backing up the information on your PC bring more benefits than watering the plants in your office?

Here is a manager's list of activities for a day. Look through them and prioritize them:

● First in order of imminence.
● Then in order of importance.
● Mark the fixed items with a tick.
● Then mark the items that can be moved with a star.
● Then ring the items with a high return on effort.
● Finally underline the items with a low return on effort.

Monday July 24th

● Buy Mary a birthday card for tomorrow
● Meeting 9.30 with Frank about office reorganization in September
● Prepare report for today's group meeting
● Check up on all deliveries to JR Brown Ltd for last May
● Prepare financial report for Board Meeting on Tuesday 25th August
● Job appraisal for Joe Rigoletto
● Check business mileage on all sales rep's expense forms
● Ring Eric re tennis game on Friday
● Take cats to the vet for vaccination
● Renew passport for Germany trip next week
● Lunch with Financial Director of Bide-a-Wee Ltd.
● Ring Personnel re job advertisement for new secretary
● Talk to Nigel about his lateness and poor performance

- Throw out the back numbers of *Computing in the 60s*
- Memo to all staff about canteen pricing
- E-mail French office re new Bordeaux account
- Find old memos to Beryl about job changes in mail department and send them to her

Once you have done this you can decide the order in which they need to be done and, more importantly, which ones can be displaced if there is not time to get the higher priority jobs done. Remember that this is a dynamic process; a fixed deadline task may not be very important on Monday but by Wednesday it may be vital as it has to be delivered by 14:30! One thing you will notice is that some tasks seem to stay on the list for ages and never get done because they are of a low priority. You should be ruthless about these and simply cross them off the list after a month. If they were important someone will come and tell you about them soon enough. Another point worth noting here is that none of this is going to work unless you have learnt how to say no! (See Chapter 9, Conflict Handling.)

10.3.3 Performing

Because you have prioritized your work you can now spend sensible amounts of time on one job at a time. There are four things you can do with any activity. You can *do it, throw it out, put it off* or *pass it on to someone else*. Of these the simplest is do it, as it just means that the task is done, and with a bit of luck that is the end of the matter. If you choose to put it off, because it is a low priority, then you may need to notify someone that it has been deferred and when it is likely to be done. The throw it out option can be exercised when the activity simply isn't worth bothering with, typically these include the 'let's do it if we have the time' and 'wouldn't it be nice if' activities. The fourth option is to pass the task to someone else or someone else's team. Section 10.3.5 of this chapter gives guidance on delegating activities.

Look back over the last week and come up with examples of jobs that you could have done better by choosing one of the do it, throw it out, put it off or pass it on options above. What criteria would you use to decide which is the appropriate action in a particular case?

10.3.4 Filing

Although it may seem like a low-priority task filing is an essential component of time management. If it takes you half an hour to find things every time someone asks you a question you are not going to have much time left for the things that really matter. The secret of success is efficient filing. This remains much the same whatever the technology of the filing system you use – filing trays, card indexes, hi-tech personal organizers, computer systems, diaries or even shoe boxes.

How you file things is up to you but there some obvious ways that you should consider: alphabetical for general filing; topical for projects; geographical for example, for sales territories, chronological for phone calls and accounts; and numerical for invoices and purchase orders. You should schedule time monthly and weekly (possibly daily) for keeping these files in trim. To help yourself and others you should keep an index or filing map that says what is where and how it is organized; filing systems are only of use if you can get the information back out of them quickly.

Discussion

How might you organize filing systems for different types of information? for example, for customer invoices, sales calls, calls to a computer help desk (by type of computer, application software), medical research data?

10.3.5
Delegation

When you delegate a task then you should adopt one of three strategies. First, you train them – you do the work and they learn by example for next time – this doesn't save you time but is an investment in the future. Next, you brief them – you tell them what is to be done, they question you, or you question them to make sure they understand what is to be done. This takes you some time but not as much as doing the job yourself. Finally, you can just pass the work straight on to them – only do this when you are sure that they can do it and are expecting it/have the time to do it. They then report back to you that the job is complete. Whichever of these you use the most important thing is to always recognize that the work has been done and give thanks accordingly.

It is important when you delegate something that you follow all the rules of communication laid out in Chapter 2 of the book. In this case it is vital that the people you delegate to have a clear understanding of what is required and when it needs to be done by. It is your responsibility to make sure that this is understood.

10.4
Aids to time
management

Although it has been well established that you can manage your time quite comfortably using little more than pen and paper, it is worth noting that there are a number of products available that can make the job a little easier. These fall into two types: diary-based and computer-based.

Diary-based products are freely available and typically take the form of a loose-leaf binder with dividers labelled with icons indicating the material contained in each section. The individual sections will usually include appointments (much like a conventional diary), contact list, today, notes, year planner and other items such as maps, restaurant guides, train and aircraft timetables. Their value is based on the convenience of being able to have all the day-to-day information you need ready to hand in an organized and easily accessible, easily carried book. Because they are loose leaf they can be readily updated each year, and old information taken out for archive or disposal. Ownership of one of these diary systems will not make you organized but will provide a simple mechanism to help you become organized. Such diary systems are not, as is often imagined, a product of the 1980s, but were produced in between the first and second world wars for use by army officers.

There are also a number of electronic alternatives available which provide similar functions to the diaries but with added facilities for communicating with other people using similar technology. Some of these systems are dedicated personal organizers and are small enough to fit in a jacket pocket. Others are applications which run on desk-top computers. Some are keyboard based, others use a stylus which allows you to write directly on the screen. These devices cover a wide price range and offer a wide range of facilities. Some include facilities for connection to office e-mail systems and diary management/scheduling systems, either remotely via the telephone system or locally via direct connection. As with the diary-based organizers these systems will not do the time management for you, it is still you who must plan and prioritize for yourself. They simply provide support to make it easier.

10.5 Summary

Time management is a skill which does not require complex diaries or technology. You can do it yourself, you only need to prioritize, plan, perform and make the odd list and you'll be fine.

10.6 Exercises

A weekly plan

Make a list of what you have to do/want to do next week. Prioritize these and produce a plan for the week. How might you have to change the plan if high-priority items take longer than planned?

10.6.1 Monitoring

Using your weekly plan as a starting point, monitor your plan over a four-week period. See how you need to modify the plan over time. Also see if there are any activities that never get done. If you have any of these, ask yourself if they need to be done at all, or is someone else doing them for you. At the end of the time write a report indicating what you have observed about the pattern of your working/personal life and how you might change that pattern for the better.

10.6.2 Benefits of time management

What are the benefits of time management and why is it important for communication skills? Give examples from your own experience of how poor time management has contributed to bad business communication.

11   Working in teams

'The power of a waterfall is nothing but a lot of drips working together.'
Anon.
'Never confuse motion with action.' Ernest Hemingway

11.1 Introduction

With the exception of those who become hermits, or are abandoned on a desert island, we all work in a team at some time or other. Even supposedly solitary occupations such as writing books are more team efforts than they might appear to be – you have to deal with editors, PR and marketing people, you may have to be involved in research. For teams to be effective, and for people to enjoy working in them, good communications skills are essential. This chapter deals with the communications issues that are specific to teams and covers how different roles within a team require different communication skills, and although it is applicable in non-team working, how to approach meetings and how to make them effective.

It is a human trait to work in a group. We are used to it from birth – the first group we live within is the family. We then go through our education in groups – why should business be any different? Many people like shared responsibility, shared problems and shared success.

Shared skills and experience make it more likely that a successful decision will be made, or a task completed more effectively.

People in a group very often motivate each other far more successfully than a single leader can.

Group decisions (though usually more effective) always take longer than individual decisions, and the group sometimes has such fun that business goals get lost.

11.2 Communication within teams

Is the communication cycle any different when we work within teams or groups? Not really, we still need to aim, encode, transmit, receive, decode and respond just as effectively. However, there are several special factors that enter the equation when we work in groups.

Discussion

Why do you think people so often work in groups as opposed to working alone? What benefits to you think that group working can bring to an organization? What might be the disadvantages of working in a group?

11.3 How teams get together

When a group of people form a team, they go through a set of behaviours that help to form the team into a viable working unit. First, everyone tends to mill about, getting to know each other and all asking the same sorts of questions: What are we here for? What are we supposed to do? Why are we joining together? This is called the 'forming stage'. What the team needs at this point is a strong direction. They need to know what the team's objectives are, what they are expected to achieve as a team, and where the team is going.

The communication needs of a team at this point are quite clear. Objectives must be set, discussed and accepted. Individual task areas need to be defined and agreed, time scales need to be set and standards must be clearly understood. This should be done both verbally and in writing. Whoever is leader at this point does not need to spend time making friends – this is not what the team needs at this point – what is needed is clear direction, clear tasking and clear organization. The logistics of team meetings and communication standards need to be set up at this point as well; where shall they meet? When? How often? How will they communicate? What is the team called? Who are they responsible to as a team? What resources do they have at their disposal? and so on.

Once the team members know where they are going they then start to ask questions like, 'Who is leader here? What is my position within the team? What is my status here?' This is called the 'storming' stage and it can be quite uncomfortable, with people jostling for position and often challenging the person who is seen as the leader at the beginning of the team's formation. Again, this is quite natural, and until individuals know and are satisfied with their position within the team then they will not move forward as a team member.

At this stage the communication needs of the team are also clear – they must be able to discuss and express themselves. The team leader at this point should act as umpire and chairperson, should be available for consultation and mediation, but not be too directive or autocratic or the team will probably turn on him or her and fight!

Now the team begins to join together and a set of 'norms' for team behaviour arises. Norms are the unspoken and unwritten rules that the team uses to keep itself together and feeling comfortable. These may be things like the sort of clothes they wear, whether the team is punctual or unpunctual, how they address each other, whether they all go out for a drink after work, how much people tell each other about their personal life, how formal or informal they are at meetings, and how much information is shared. This is called the 'norming' stage and is not over until the team feels that each of them knows how to behave and agrees with those behaviours. Indeed, team norms are sometimes so strong that if an individual member refuses to abide by them then the team may well expel that individual.

At this point the leader should be a participant rather than a dictator. It is generally true that the leader's behaviour will influence the team (for instance if the leader is punctual, the team is usually punctual, if the leader is rude to team members, the team will be rude to each other and the leader and so on) but it is the team that is ultimately the creator of norms rather than the leader.

After a team has formed, stormed and normed then, and only then, can it move on to the most successful stage of team behaviour – performing.

Discussion

What group 'norms' have you observed within your team?

Have you observed norms in other groups, for instance different departments within your organization, other families, social clubs?

11.4
Basic composition of successful teams

When teams get together, each person within the team fulfils a double purpose. First they need to complete and perform the tasks that the team has been formed to do (like running a machine, programming a computer, delivering goods). These utilize the business or intellectual skills that we bring to the team.

Second, they need to take a *team role*. These roles refer to the behaviours that the team members exhibit. These are not particularly to do with completing the team's tasks, more to do with the successful working of the team itself (things like leading the team, motivating the team, making sure that the team is keeping to schedule, keeping the team on track). These roles are our natural and preferred ways of working together, and we are usually capable of taking more than one role.

Every successful team needs to have people within them who fulfil the following roles for some or all of the time. Even teams of three will need these behaviours within it if they are to succeed.

11.4.1 Leaders

Without a leader a team is directionless – they never get beyond the 'storming' stage and very quickly lose motivation. The original team leader (when the team is forming/storming and norming) may not be the ultimate leader when the team is performing. As the tasks of the team change different leaders may well arise due to technical needs, influencing needs or resourcing needs. A good leader will always move aside when it is necessary.

11.4.2 Opponents

It may seem strange to need opponents within a team, but without healthy opposition a team becomes too obedient to the leader, never questions the reasons for their actions or refines the process they use to reach their goals. If you are a small team, you should try to have 'devil's advocate' sessions to test the validity of what you and your leader are doing.

11.4.3 Supporters

Obviously you need supporters – they are the ones that actually get the work done, however – too much slavish obedience can be dangerous.

11.4.4 Outsiders

Often the hardest team members to understand, outsiders seem to be uninvolved and this can de-motivate the rest of the team. But the outsider is the team's quality control, they keep a sense of proportion and look at the team's impact on the rest of the company. If your team does not naturally have an outsider try to bring one in to give their input.

11.5
Team think or
group think

'Group think' or 'team think' is rather like a virus that affects apparently successful groups. It was identified in 1972 by Janis and Mann. They identified a pattern of behaviour which leads to extremely poor-quality decisions and outcomes – and eventually (although the team may not be fully aware that this is happening) the distancing of the team's thinking from the realities of their surroundings, leading to failure to meet the objectives that the team was set. The main cause of team think is poor communication, both within the team and between the team and the rest of the company.

Under the following conditions the team-think syndrome is likely to occur:

- Where the team is very well bonded and enjoys working together.
- Where the team does not get any outside criticism.
- Where the team leader is particularly strong and the team follows his/her lead.
- Where the team does not make alternative plans.
- Where the team does not look critically at their actions.
- Where there is pressure to make fast decisions.

11.5.1
The symptoms of
team think

Self censorship

Each member censors any doubts they may have in order to get group agreement.

False sense of unanimity

Each member assumes that everyone (except themself) is in agreement. This means that they believe that because other members of the team are silent they are in agreement with the rest.

Direct pressure on dissenters

Anyone expressing doubts is pressured to conform.

Peaceguards

Certain team members try to stop others from raising objections.

False sense of invulnerability

The team comes to believe that it is invulnerable. This is shown by great optimism (usually false) and an increase in risk-taking. It is as if the team believes that it is all-powerful and beyond reproach.

Justification

Team members justify any action that the team feels it needs to do.

Deliberate ignoring of ethical considerations

Team members deliberately fail to take account of ethical considerations, feeling that anything they do is morally justified.

'Cartoonising'

Anyone who is in competition with the team, likely to criticise the team or react negatively to the team is turned into a 'cartoon character' and treated as though they are unreal. The team is likely to dismiss them as too wicked, stupid or weak to have any effect on the team.

**11.5.2
The cure**

As you can see from the above causes and symptoms, most of the problems can be cured by effective communication. Most of the sick team's beliefs are based on unchecked assumptions and lack of communication with people outside the team as well as lack of communication with other team members.

To cure team think you need to listen to the 'outsiders' in the group – they usually have a much more dispassionate view of the team's behaviours. Appoint an official cynic who will voice doubts about the team's performance and challenge the team's decisions

Hold 're-think' meetings. As soon as the team has seemed to reach a consensual decision on what seems to be the best course of action, the decision should be put off until a re-think meeting has been held. In this meeting each member voices their doubts as vividly as possible and re-thinks the whole decision before making any choice.

You need to hold contingency planning sessions, where the team should be encouraged to think about all the things that could go wrong in a project or course of action. Contingency plans should be prepared to cope with these. External experts may need to be brought in to advise the team. It is too easy to forget the realities of the outside world and think only within the team's perspective. Finally, before any team decision is acted upon the team should ask itself 'Is this reasonable behaviour? What will we gain from this? What will others think of us? What will the impact of our actions be on the rest of the company?'

**11.6
Leadership**

So what is leadership? Donald H. McGannon defined it as being 'action, not position'. In other words the job title is not what makes you a team leader it is what you say and do and the example you set. Advice on leadership comes from General George S. Patton: 'Never tell people how to do things. Tell them what to do and they will surprize you with their ingenuity.' This is something that I've seen time and time again with techies who are put in charge of a programming team. Instead of setting clear goals and objectives for their team they spend ages looking at their code and telling them how they would have done it. This has the effect of not only wasting everyone's time but also creates considerable animosity between the leader and the led.

One of the first skills that must be acquired to become a successful team leader is that of setting objectives. You cannot expect people to do a job for you unless they are clear what they are supposed to be doing. They must know what the team and individual objectives are.

The acronym, SMART (Simple, Measurable, Achievable, Realistic/ Resource, Timetable) helps you evaluate objectives. 'To have your team paint the Forth Road bridge blue by Tuesday' is simple: it is measurable (it will have turned blue), it isn't achievable using current technology, you would need immense resources not just a few workers (so it isn't realistic), and the timetable is ludicrous. Therefore having this as an objective would not work. This is a trivial example, but the same measurement can be applied to any team goal; nothing demotivates people faster than being made to work hard at something that can never be completed. Objectives may be difficult and challenging but they should be possible and clearly defined.

Once you have checked out the objectives against the SMART test you must establish how you, in your role as team leader, will implement it. Rudyard Kipling's 'I keep six honest serving men (they taught me all I knew); their names are What and Why and When, and How and Where and Who' can serve you well here. For example, the following questions are typical of those you should ask yourself. You will be able to think of more yourself along the same theme:

- What resource is needed to get the work done? What are the external dependencies?
- Why do we need to do this? Why is it important?
- When do we need to start/complete the work? When do we need to tell other teams that we have completed it?
- How do I motivate the team to do it? How do we measure it? How will it affect other objectives?
- Where do I get the resources? Where will they sit?
- Who is going to help me? Who needs to know what actions I am taking? Who will benefit from the objective being achieved?

This may seem to be time consuming but like preparation time spent before cooking a meal it makes a tremendous difference to the finished result and to the amount of dirty pans (or plans) left over at the end.

Once the team objectives are established then it is possible to define those for the individual team members. The SMART criteria apply in exactly the same way. Each individual must know what they are going to do, how it is to be measured, that it is something that can be done in the time, and that the resources they require are available to them.

**11.6.1
Team dynamics**

Another area for team leaders to be aware of is that of team dynamics. The diagram below shows the basic dynamics.

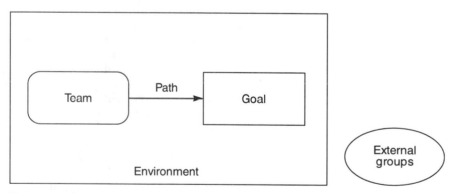

Figure 11.1 Team dynamics

Team

Who you work with. Factors to consider include: size, maturity, skill set, personalities, roles within the team, leadership style, experience of team members, expectations, motivation, and reward.

Goal

The team's objective (remember SMART), how it is defined, timescales, how each team member is to contribute to achieving the goal.

Path

Methods used to achieve goal, who does what, use of internal and external resources, motivation process, reporting and delegation processes.

Environment	The world in which the team operates, the department, division etc. of the company, politics, standards, shared resources, attitude of people outside the team to the project, desk space, computer resources, effect of goals on this environment.
External groups	Other groups which may affect the team, groups which have goals that conflict with the teams, groups who have staff seconded to the team, groups which compete for the same resources.

11.6.2 Summary

- Are team objectives clearly set?
- Is it SMART?
- Are individual goals defined?
- What, Why, When, How, Where, and Who.

11.7 Meetings

'The length of a meeting rises in direct proportion to the square of the number of people present.' Eileen Shanahan

An inevitable fact of working life is the necessity to attend meetings. Business revolves around them for they provide the most convenient method for broadcasting and forming decisions. We've all experienced the awfulness of a bad meeting rather more often than we would like, but that doesn't mean that all meetings have to be that way.

The most important item is the agenda, without which you are sunk. Even if it is just scribble on a white board, it is vital. Before you can develop an agenda you need to have an objective for the meeting. If you can't think of one, cancel the meeting, as there is no virtue in having one just because there has always been one every Friday since anyone can remember. The objective, the purpose of the meeting, also allows you to decide who needs to be there. It is no use having a technical progress meeting with only the accounts department represented. Ideally only people who are actively involved with the agenda items should be present. Additional sitters-in only drag the proceedings out. However, you may need people for political reasons, and these may be left out only at your peril.

Next, you must find a suitable location for the meeting – a desk in a busy open-plan office is not a good idea. You must make sure that all the participants can make it; try and give them at least a week's notice, as it considerably improves your chances of getting the people you need there. Remember to tell them where and when it is, and explain what is expected of them so that they can prepare. It is no use asking someone to provide a complex analysis of downsizing strategies for a multi-national PLC at ten minutes' notice – give them at least a couple of hours!

Now for the meeting itself. The value of a good chair cannot be underestimated. The role of the chair includes making sure that the attendees keep to the agenda, that debates do not get 'rat-holed' into in-depth technical issues, that discussions do not turn into abusive rows, and that decisions are summarized so that everyone is clear what the consensus is. It is also very important to record decisions and actions for future reference, so there is no doubt in a week's time as to who should be doing what (people have amazingly fickle memories when they haven't done something they said they were going to do). Finally, it is good practice to end the meeting with a 'what next' even if it is only to determine when the next meeting should be.

Having done all these things you have won much more than half the battle and are well on the way to having a productive, and hopefully short, meeting. If you are not running the meeting then you can at least make sure that you ask for an agenda, establish what is expected of you, prepare beforehand and know when and where it is.

**11.7.1
Summary**

- Have an agenda.
- Make sure people know when and where the meeting is.
- Make sure people know what they need to do before the meeting.
- Explain why they are invited.
- Record actions and decisions.
- Agree next steps.
- Keep it relevant.

**11.8
Summary**

Working in teams is the norm in most businesses and organizations. Understanding how teams work and how you can be effective in them is a useful, practically an essential, skill. Many modern industrial practices depend on the effective operation of teams, for example 'quality circles' where people work together within a group constantly reviewing each other's work in team meetings, searching for improvements. Concentrating on team communications and roles and how they interact will help you gain a better understanding of what goes on in teams and how you can work more successfully in them.

**11.9
Exercises**

**11.9.1
A new team**

You have just been seconded to a small team of four who have been asked to design a new office layout. You have never met any of the other team members before. You are a specialist in computer networks. There is to be a team briefing this afternoon. What do you need to know in order to work effectively in the team? Draw up a list of questions that you would like to ask the team leader.

**11.9.2
A celebration**

You have been asked to organize a celebration party for sixty people. You know that you will need a team of people to help you to do this.

- What tasks will the team need to do in order to organize the party effectively?
- What information does the team need in order to start working?
- Write an agenda for the first team meeting.
- Prepare the opening paragraphs of the team briefing.

11.9.3
The stockroom

You are leading a team of nine who are responsible for the stockroom of a large retail company selling electrical goods. What objectives would you set for your team? Check that these objectives are SMART.

12 Teleworking

'Be it ever so humble, there's no place like home for wearing what you like.' George Ade, 1901.

Teleworker: *someone who works from a home base making use of some form of telecommunications to contact the outside world in the course of their business.*

12.1 Introduction

Teleworking, that is working from home and communicating via phone lines by fax, voice, vision or data modem, has been with us since the 1970s when it was pioneered by companies such as Xerox. It is one of those ideas that seems to have everything going for it but has never taken off as fast as expected. An information technology analogy might be with the use of colour. The technology for colour has been about since the late 1960s, but it wasn't until the advent of PC-based GUIs (graphical-user interfaces) which took over from character-based technology, that demand shot up and prices plummeted. Within a couple of years of this, colour became commonplace. It is no coincidence that this was rapidly followed by affordable desktop colour printing.

Teleworking was at a similar point in its evolution in 1995. In 1994 it was calculated that fewer than 0.5 per cent of all employees were teleworkers – less than 1 in 200. However, this percentage is much higher among journalists, service engineers, technical authors, illustrators, sales staff and IT workers who have been in the vanguard of this way of working. In addition, the growing number of telecottages in the UK, and the active marketing drives by both computer manufacturers and telecommunications suppliers, provide further encouragement for this type of working.

However, teleworking is by no means restricted to information technology-based industries. Examples include financial services, telemarketing, and car servicing. Consequently, it is not unreasonable to expect that most people reading this book will find themselves involved in some form of teleworking during their working lives.

Discussion

What are the environmental benefits of teleworking? Why do you think that the Information Technology industry in particular is in favour of teleworking?

**12.2
What is
teleworking?**

A teleworker is anyone who spends part, or all, of their time working from a home base and communicating with their employer/customers using some form of telecommunication equipment. At one end of the scale this can mean someone who does all their work at home communicating with the outside world using a telephone. At the other end of the scale it includes people who have sophisticated equipment with high-speed data communication links that enable them to share information with their home office and other colleagues. It may also provide them with the means to have teleconferencing – sound and vision – links with other people so that they can hold meetings without having to leave their home. Although there is quite a range of price for the equipment involved, the top-end of the range is still an investment considerably less than the cost of a new, bottom-of-the-range small car. Employers who are keen on teleworking will often provide such equipment (it can also be leased) so an ever-increasing proportion of the working population will have this technology within reach.

Electronic mail at workgroup, corporate, national and international level is well established and emergent technologies have supplied, more or less, affordable teleconferencing with combined sound, vision and data services.

**12.2.1
Hot desking**

Running alongside teleworking and home working is 'hot-desking'. This recognizes that we have a social need to meet to exchange views, have progress meetings, motivate each other and so on. In this, people have a mixed working pattern where they are home-based perhaps two or three days a week and office-based for the remainder. Buildings are equipped only for so many staff being in the office at a given time. This has communications implications for people who do not have their own territory in the office, but use whatever workstation is available to them. Unlike a conventional office where you can leave a note on someone's desk, in the hot-desking environment you have to leave notes either electonically or using a 'pigeon hole' system. The implications of hot desking mainly involve the architectural needs of office buildings: the emphasis will move towards meeting-space at the expense of dedicated working space.

**12.3
Benefits of
teleworking**

In the early 1990s teleworking made global news as a result of bad weather and earthquakes in that home of the freeway, California, USA. Many high-tech companies found that they were able to get themselves up and running once the phone and computer links had been restored long before the competition, who were reliant on roads being repaired before their staff could clock in. Californian environmental pressure groups also saw a chance to curb some of the excesses of the motorcar; the result has been a significant boost for teleworking.

The benefits of teleworking are many:

For the Employer
- Financial
- Flexibility

Specific examples include the reduction of overhead and direct-staff costs, particularly when coupled with contract working. There are also potential savings in equipment costs for PCs, faxes and photocopiers, though this is very dependent on the pattern of working (you may end up having to have more of these items, rather than less).

Another point concerns accessibility. Home-based staff are much more open to being called out of normal hours to get something done that would normally wait until the next day in a more conventional working environment.

For the employee

- Quality of life
- Flexibility
- Financial

Specific examples include reduced travelling times and the option to move away from the more expensive parts of the country with the chance of a better place to live. The latter can be limited by the necessity to make occasional site visits for meetings; desert islands aren't quite practical yet. Flexibility in working hours means single parents can take on work that might otherwise be unprofitable after paying for crèche or child-minding fees. Financial benefits result from reduced travelling and subsistence costs – you can eat more cheaply at home!

External benefits

The principal benefit of teleworking comes in the form of reduced traveling and consequent reduction in pollution associated with transport. Even when people take advantage of being home based to live further away from their workplace this is still a major benefit. One long car journey a week, where the car is running at its optimum temperature and therefore least polluting, is much better than five short ones where the vehicle is putting out the maximum concentration of pollutants.

Similarly, there are the indirect benefits relating to lower numbers of road casualties from lower overall road mileage, lower incidence of air-quality related diseases, and potential for reduced stress.

Discussion

What environmental benefits might you expect to come from teleworking? Are these benefits absolute or might there be associated drawbacks?

12.4 Disadvantages of teleworking

Nothing comes without its downside, and teleworking is no exception. The costs of teleworking are by no means all associated with material factors. Social issues are a major consideration as well.

12.4.1 For the employer

There are concerns about management control with teleworking, which makes itself felt in two ways. There are still many managers who don't trust staff they can't see. It also requires different skills to manage distributed project teams and many companies do not feel that the techniques have yet to prove themselves. These problems can all be solved. Indeed examples abound of successful implementations of teleworking, notably in journalism and companies such as Rank Xerox, ICL, BT and The Digital Equipment Corporation.

12.4.2 For the employee

Social

The social aspects influencing teleworking revolve around the potential to become isolated. Many people meet partners through working, so the scope for this is far less for the full-time teleworker. A recent survey showed that social interaction came second only to money as the reason for working, ahead of job satisfaction and prospects. A solution to this is to combine teleworking with hot desking. One of my happiest contracts involved home-based working three days a week with site visits the other two, where I felt that I got the best of both worlds. Coincidentally, this could be part of the solution to the remote management problems that many companies fear.

Facilities

Working from home brings another problem, in the form of office facilities. You need to have a dedicated office space which is big enough for the work that you need to do, typically a PC, a fax and a printer at a minimum. You also need filing space, room for manuals and reference material – a dedicated space of about three metres by two metres. If you live in a one bedroomed flat this can be tricky. Furthermore, you need to be able to work in this room, which means that partners and children have to realize that just because someone is at home doesn't mean they are there to play.

This can require creative thinking. One parent agreed that for fifteen minutes every two hours he would be exclusively at the disposal of the rug rats (aka children) and they could play any game they wanted. Apparently this worked out well in practice although it took a couple of weeks to establish the routine.

These facilities cost money. Starting from scratch may be fairly expensive, with software costs being potentially greater than hardware in the long term. However, permanent employee teleworkers often get the equipment provided by the employer.

Health and safety are also considerations. When at the employer's premises, they are responsible for your safety, overseeing that proper working practices are followed etc. However, when you are at home you are responsible for your own safety. Certainly, there needs to be some common company policy to deal with this.

Financial

Homeworkers have traditionally been poorly paid, if you go by the example of the exported sweatshop approach common in the rag trade. For 'professional' workers, mainly in IT and the media, this is less of a problem. Given that most people involved in teleworking will probably only be home-based two or three days a week they are going to be treated much as traditional employees and pay rates should end up being those that the market supports.

If there are financial drawbacks to home working then they are the ones usually affecting freelance workers – cashflow may be affected by slow payment; forward planning is more difficult with short-term contracts and unpaid time may need to be scheduled for finding new work. The traditional support that people have been used to when working in an office (secretarial, accountancy, office upkeep and so on) becomes the duty of the homeworker and this will inevitably affect the volume of the output for each day.

Career structure

Permanent staff can fear that if they are not seen their career prospects may suffer and they will lose out financially. The solution to this lies with the adoption of suitable management methods. These already exist. It is critical mass that is required to make them commonplace.

12.4.3 External

The reduction in the need for large-scale office accommodation can bring with it reduction in employment for the staff associated with running the buildings.

**12.5
Communications
aspects**

Communication skills for teleworkers are vital. People working this way are dependent on their communication skills to get instructions as to what they are expected to do and to exchange information with the outside world. Anyone working in this way must pay particular attention to improving these skills.

There are four core skills that are vital for anyone working from home, whether they are using computer technology or not: correspondence, time management, team working, and telephone skills. These are covered in Chapters 5, 10, 11, and subsection 12.6 of this chapter. Those using computing technology will also need to be familiar with the use of e-mail, which is the subject of Chapter 6.

It is doubly important in a teleworking environment that communication works first time. It is not always possible to go back and ask for clarification if you aren't sure about something – the person may not be available for a few days, so you need to pay significant attention to your communication skills, and ideally get training in this. Companies should make an investment in telecommunications equipment to make communications as near to those experienced by staff working in a traditional office environment as possible.

Discussion

Why are communication skills so important for teleworkers and others who work from a home base?

**12.6
Telephone
techniques**

By the nature of their work, home-based staff will inevitably spend a considerable amount of time communicating by phone.

12.6.1
Using the telephone

How you use the telephone has a major effect on how you, your office/ organization are perceived. Despite the fact that we use the telephone every day, many people, particularly at work, are unbelievably bad at it. It is a chastening experience to listen to the difference between one of your colleagues (or yourself) when talking to a friend 'Hello, Harry, how're you doing? Did you hear about Jane and the giant penguin in accounts?' and when answering someone else's phone (after at least ten rings) 'Yes? Who? He's not here. Bye'.

It is really very simple to do it right. When you pick up the phone say who you are, and try and sound pleased about it, adding good morning/afternoon as appropriate. You should also aim to answer the phone within two to three rings as a maximum. There was once a database designer whose attitude to the telephone left much to be desired. If the phone on the desk next to his rang he ignored it and waited for it to stop. When asked why he said, 'I'm not a secretary. I'm technical.' It remains to be established which technical skills prevented his arm from moving, ear from listening and voice from speaking. Answering the phone is not demeaning, it is professional. If nothing else, answer the phone for others as you would like them to answer for yourself. Better still, take messages and pass them on, or if you can help, try and sort out the caller's problem yourself.

When you have to divert people it is important that you tell them why they are being diverted and to whom. You should also give them the number to which they are being transferred in case of problems with the transfer so they can ring in themselves if necessary without having to start back at square one again.

Equally important is taking messages: as a minimum you should record who rang, their number, who they wished to get in touch with and the time of the message. In addition you should try and find out what they rang about and when they need a response by. You can also add value by telling the caller when the person they want will be contactable and setting their expectations for when they can expect a response. Finally, it is no use taking a message unless you make sure it is delivered.

Figure 12.1 shows a typical call logging sheet. These can be purchased from most stationers and most organizations will have their own version of this in the form of a tear-off pad.

Message from:	To:
Company:	Phone number:
Called	Will call again
Return your call	Please call back
Message	
Taken by:	Time/Date:

Figure 12.1 Call recording form

Telephone checklist

- Say who you are
- Be helpful
- Be positive
- Sound enthusiastic
- Take messages (and deliver them)

Discussion

What makes you most annoyed by people who you phone, and are phoned by? How might it be done better?

12.7 Remote management

In addition to these core skills it is important to be aware of the specific management issues that apply for people working from home. Fortunately the basics of remote management were determined long before technology made it practical for a wide range of staff – the classic example being that of managing the sales rep.

A manager's attitude to remote workers is the basis for a good or bad relationship. If the manager feels that working from home is a soft option, and that home workers are basically shiftless and untrustworthy then it is probable that the majority of the communication between the two will consist of the manager checking that work is being done, and the home worker feeling constantly monitored and tacitly criticized. If the manager believes that the home worker is productive, self-motivated and honest, then the communication between them is likely to be one of sharing information, working out better ways to achieve joint goals and mutual help.

The physical distance between the manager and the home worker leads to all kinds of misconceptions. Figure 12.2 shows the thought process that might occur when there is insufficient contact between manager and worker.

What the home worker thinks ...	What the manager thinks ...
As long as I do the job I don't need to report in every day	The home worker isn't working
If the manager doesn't ring me there's nothing I need to know	If the home worker doesn't ring me, there's nothing he/she needs to know
I hate to disturb the manager, so I won't ring	I won't disturb the home worker, so I won't ring
I must solve all my problems by myself	No phone calls, no problems
No one ever tells me how well I'm doing	He/she knows how well he/she's doing
I need feedback on how I'm doing the job	He/she's always done a good job
I need criticism from time to time	Criticism over the phone is difficult to handle
I need to discuss the job with a colleague	The home worker has his/her family to talk to

Figure 12.2

Figure 12.3 shows what can be done by the home worker and the manager to alleviate the possible pitfalls of isolation, alienation, demotivation and misunderstanding.

Managerial actions	Home worker actions
Schedule (and keep to it) regular, frequent telephone contact. Pick a suitable time and stick to it. Have an agenda so that at the very least these things are covered: • Update from manager on progress on the project/job in hand • Any changes affecting the home worker • Any new information that affects the home worker • Any difficulties, present or expected • Any update on news about the company, colleagues, other projects that affect the homeworker • Congratulations or corrections	Schedule (and keep to it) regular, frequent telephone contact. Pick a suitable time and stick to it. Have an agenda that covers at least these things: • Update from home worker on progress on the project/job in hand • Any changes affecting this job, yourself or your manager • Any new information that is relevant • Any difficulties, present or expected • Update on news affecting you and the job • Any requests for help
Exceptionally clear planning and tasking	Ask for clarification of anything that is unclear
Consultative decision making and planning	Consultative decision making and planning
Future planning	Future planning
Problem-solving sessions	Problem-solving sessions
Face-to-face meetings when possible	Face-to-face meetings when possible
Organised 'get togethers' with colleagues and remote workers	Contact with colleagues and other remote workers involved in the project/tasks in hand
Clear recognition of a job well done	Critical self evaluation of projects and tasks completed
Efficient recording of all projects and details for each home worker. These records to be available for anyone deputizing for the manager in the manager's absence	Efficient records of all projects and tasks
Escalation procedures so the manager can delegate the task of managing when he/she is unavailable	Clear understanding of escalation procedures
Regular feedback	Regular feedback
Open communication	Open communication – no harbouring of grudges
Belief in and encouragement for the remote worker's ability to organise and fulfil tasks	Ability to put forward and defend own ideas
Clear management structure	Always go through your manager – don't go above his/her head or behind his/her back

Figure 12.3

If there is a genuine, and organised effort to keep regularly in touch with each other, and if the relationship is one of trust and mutual help, then there is no reason why remote workers should feel any less involved with their managers than the staff in the same office as the manager. Remember out of sight should never mean out of mind.

12.8 Summary

Teleworking is an increasingly common way of working – the benefits to both employers and suppliers of teleworking are too great for it to be otherwise. During their working life almost all people working in business can expect to have some part of their time spent working in this way. It is unlikely that more than a small percentage of the population will become full-time teleworkers even if the majority become part-time ones.

From the viewpoint of communications teleworking demands a wide range of skills and practices, in particular e-mail, correspondence, time management and team working.

12.9 Exercises

Discussion

12.9.1 Communications problems

Will teleworking be a source of well-paid work with an improved quality of life and a better environment, or will it result in isolated low-paid high-tech workers with little or no security of employment?

What are the communications problems for teleworkers and their managers? What approach might be taken to reduce or eliminate such problems?

12.9.2 Risks and benefits

Consider the main benefits to an employer of teleworking. What are the potential risks of this to the employee?

12.9.3 The hifi repair company

You are the manager of a TV and hifi repair company. You are considering changing from having all your staff based in a central office to having them all based at home, except for a small number needed to do larger repairs which cannot be made on site. How would you go about persuading your staff that this was a good idea? What savings would you expect to gain as a result of this change? How might you ensure that staff did not feel isolated and, at the same time, ensure that you could be confident they were doing the work they were supposed to?

12.9.4 The telephone campaign

Why is telephone technique so important? How would you go about implementing a campaign within an organisation to improve the way the telephone is answered? How would you measure if there had been an improvement or not?

Sample completed exercises

These answers are only guidelines. They are there to help you to expand your own understanding of the subject matter. In many cases there are no definitive answers to the questions posed in the chapters.

Chapter 2 Effective communication

Types of information

a, c, f, g, i, j.

Discussion on language

Morse code, the special alphabet that air crew use to communicate (alpha, bravo, charlie, delta. . . .), exact medical terminology, glossary of terms are some.

Chapter 3 Presentations

Why do people make presentations in your organization?

Most people think of presentations as being a formal process, often involving sales messages or company messages. In fact the majority of presentations in an organization are to do with updating your colleagues or managers on progress, telling and showing people how to use equipment, outlining projects, making a case for resources and so on. A presentation can be defined as a structured communication where you put your point across to one or more people.

Exercise 1

A 20-minute presentation to an audience of six people

'Good morning. For those of you who do not know me I am XXX, the Sales Manager of the SE Area, based in our Basingstoke office (*contact information, credibility*). For the next 20 minutes (*expectations*) I shall be covering the sales results for my area over the last six months (*what the presentation is about*). These have been excellent, but if we are to continue winning our market share I need some help from you (*objective, benefits, understanding audience concerns, conclusion*). Over the last six months we have opened up three new major accounts, two of them in market areas we have never penetrated before. We have also introduced two new products to the marketplace and kept our cost of sale 10 per cent below our targets (*background to the presentation, audience concerns*). I am also aware that we are about to launch an important new product, and my team has made plans for this – I will be presenting these plans later (*active listening*).

'I will also be covering the following points: sales booked to date; potential in our new accounts; expected ordering levels; customer feedback on the range of products we sell; projected sales for the next six months; and finally, the logistical help our team needs to fulfil the potential in these accounts (*expectations, agenda*).

'Before I begin the presentation I'd like to give you a remarkable statistic. The SE sales team has achieved 200 per cent over budget – and it is the smallest sales team in the company (*attention grabber*).

Exercise 2

Open day

- What will you put on the title slide?
- What are your objectives?
- Do they know who you are? Your name, job title and contact information should be on the title slide.
- Do they know why you are giving this presentation?
- What is the background to the presentation?
- What is your conclusion? (Remember – you want that grant!)
- How will you show that you understand their concerns? Are they interested in your services, your terms of trading, the value you are adding to the community?
- What's in it for them (benefits)?
- Set the scene for the presentation (the agenda should be on a slide or a handout).
- How will you grab their attention?
- When will you finish? Will there be question time? Will there be handouts (the local government officers seem interested in these)?
- How will you encourage them to listen actively?

Chapter 4 Reports and proposals

Chapter 5 Correspondence

Why is it important to get the right form of address on a letter

If you misspell people's names or get their job title wrong it suggests (perfectly reasonably) that you can't be bothered to do your research. People absolutely hate it when their names are misspelt and they are unlikely to take anything you say seriously if you do this.

If you aren't sure just how people like to be addressed then ring up the company and ask the receptionist how to spell the person's name, exactly what the job title is and check the address.

Chapter 6 Electronic mail

E-mail versus paper discussion

It is a matter of deciding how urgent the message is and if it is necessary to have proof of its receipt. For example, the Company Pension Scheme needs to be read by all employees and it is therefore sensible to send it as a 'registered' e-mail that sends a message back to the sender to confirm that it has been received. However, it would only need to be a low priority message as it would probably not matter to a week or two when it was dealt with. Similarly you would use 'registered' e-mail for the Project Review meeting, but you might need to mark it urgent if a speedy reply was needed – flagging the urgency to the recipient.

Traditional paper-based mail systems can be marked urgent or given priorities. However, they do not have the visual impact of e-mail priorities on a computer screen. Similarly the only way for someone to guarantee receipt of a message is to have someone else physically collect a receipt from the recipient. This is time-consuming and expensive compared to the electronic alternative and is consequently unlikely to be used except in rare cases in the normal office environment.

E-mail security discussion

Discussion should include such points as: physical access security to terminals – making sure people do not leave them logged onto the system when they are away from their desks; restricting access by visitors to locations where terminals are located etc.; password security – making people change their passwords frequently, never writing passwords down, never telling them to other staff – personal encryption of sensitive material so that system operators cannot get at information they are not privileged to see; not printing out sensitive information and leaving it where it can readily be seen by others; ensuring that e-mails cannot be removed from the building on computer disks etc.

Where systems are connected to external communication systems such as the Internet then it becomes even more important to police systems to ensure that sensitive information cannot be accessed from the outside world. This is a major problem and is more dependent on the security attitudes of the people involved than a technological barrier. However, links to the outside world can be monitored so that at least the person responsible for the breach of security stands a good chance of being tracked down. Sometimes it is simpler to have links with the outside world that have no physical connection with the internal E-mail systems thus providing a physical barrier between the inside and outside world that can be readily controlled. The importance of these problems of security should not be undervalued – there have been numerous incidents where either direct fraud or the loss of vital competitive company information has taken place at severe cost to the companies concerned.

Discussion on international e-mail

Points raised in discussion might include: replacement of surface post for letters and basic business communications due to higher speeds and lower costs with consequent loss in revenue to the postal companies – leading to lower employment and smaller profit margins; consequential loss of/ increased cost of traditional services to those without access to computer systems. Telecommunications organizations could expect to benefit providing that they are successful competitors in the race to supply the 'carrier' services that the e-mail system uses such as the telephone network, cable TV networks etc.

In terms of employment, those without access to e-mail could find themselves cut off in much the same way as those without access to fax machines or telephones are now. As the use of such technology becomes more and more widespread this disadvantage can only increase.

Chapter 7 Interviews and appraisals

Question

The interviewer and interviewee usually know very little about each other. Although the CV and job advertisement give a certain amount of information, this information needs to be checked in a face to face situation. We tend to base our judgements of people on experiences we have had in the past – and although this may be of some use in evaluating hard facts we need to recognise that when meeting new people we are, in effect, starting with a blank sheet.

The successful 'encode, decode' process depends on understanding the way the receiver will interpret the message sent, but this can be difficult if the only information we have is from the CV or the job/company description.

If questions are carelessly phrased they may lead to inaccurate or limited answers. If answers are carelessly given this may lead to faulty impressions.

Assumptions will seriously interfere with the clarity of the communication – the interviewer should be particularly careful not to 'label' or categorize the candidate. If a false impression is given on either side then the chances of a smooth induction of the new candidate into the company will be small.

The key points for an interviewer and an interviewee

- Planning
- Listening skills
- Questioning skills
- Creating rapport
- Keeping an open mind
- Checking information
- Judgement
- Patience

Chapter 8
Negotiation

8.4.1. Exercise 1 – Open Questions

1 'What is the price range for this model and what extras are included in that price?'
2 'What are your delivery services and what guarantees of arrival do you give?'
3 'What will be my holiday entitlement and will you honour arrangements I have already made?'
4 'Would you tell me about training and development in your company.'
5 'What discounts would you offer on 5, 10, 15 or 20 units?'
6 'What sort of payment arrangements would you be interested in?'

Best case: worst case

- Highest basic price I'll pay
- Must have these things in the basic price
- Would like to have these things and would pay for them
- Not essential to have these things

Research

Existing car prices, usual prices for repairs, reputation of the garage, what's on the market, prices of 'extras' (CDs, radios etc), insurance levels, are some.

How would you prepare for your negotiation?

First make your prioritized list: Best case/worst case, what I must have/what I'd like to have, not essential but nice/not important but can be used for bargaining.

Draw up a possible schedule.

Work out the gains that you will achieve by doing the extra work.

Cost the course price and how much it would cost for you to attend the course (temporary cover, travelling etc).

Draw up a set of guidelines that both you and your manager would need to agree in order to make the working patterns clear.

Set your attitude – 'If I do this, then you do that . . .'

Prepare a list of the things that you absolutely cannot change (the unbreakable evening engagements, the gas and electricity supplier visits, although you may be able to organise both of these for the same day).

Work out any costs that you would incur if you could not spend the time on the new house that you need to (housework help, handyman help).

Investigate the possibility of getting outside help in for sorting out the house (domestic agencies/help from friends).

Investigate the availability of temporary office help or the office junior. Find out as much as you can about exactly what the extra (overtime) work entails.

Do your sums – what is the overtime worth, could you take days in lieu after the reports are completed? Would the extra money allow you to do things to your new house that would have had to wait?

What will you need to do to make the solution work?	<ul><li>Prepare a schedule for delegation and hand-over for the tasks to be performed by the temp. or office junior.</li><li>Delegate very carefully.</li><li>Be firm but fair about making your boss stick to the agreement.</li><li>Book the domestic agency (etc).</li><li>Book the training course.</li><li>Make contingency plans.</li></ul>

Chapter 9 Conflict handling

Aggression versus assertion

Aggression = Getting your own way at the expense of others. Demanding your rights without allowing others to maintain theirs.

Assertion = Asking for what you want. Refusing to have your rights denied to you. Allowing others their rights.

Handling a conflict

Exactly whose space is it? Draw up a clear schedule and stick to it. Make sure that other people know when you will be at your desk and when the other person will be there.

Who is responsible for keeping things in order? Organise the space so that each person knows exactly where everything is. Organise places for incoming mail and messages. Have a notice board or message pad for any information that needs to be passed between you. Each person must leave the working space as they found it (tidy, in order and with all messages clearly indicated).

Message taking for the absent worker – who takes these and how are they passed on? Organise an answering service or arrange a suitable message report form that satisfies you both. Agree to answer for each other. Organise a way of getting important messages to the other person swiftly.

Timetabling – who can use the desk and when? Draw up a clear schedule and stick to it. Make sure that you keep in regular touch with the other person – never let any resentment simmer. If problems arise, deal with them as soon as possible.

Causes of Conflicts

Timing conflicts – too fast or too slow
Priority conflicts – task or people orientation
Status conflicts – where your or other's status is not acknowledged
Territorial conflicts – where your or other's space/ideas/ responsibilities are invaded

Chapter 10 Time management

High/low return on effort

The manager might examine his task list as follows:

IMMINENCE	IMPORTANCE
9.30 meeting with Frank (this morning) FIXED HIGH/ RETURN ON EFFORT	Report for today's group meeting
Group meeting preparation (this must be done before lunch) FIXED/HIGH RETURN ON EFFORT	Renew passport (trip to Germany not possible without this)
Lunch with FD of Bide-a-Wee – (today) FIXED/HIGH RETURN ON EFFORT	Talk to Nigel about lateness and poor performance (This is seriously impacting profitability)
Renew passport (this may take four days and must be ready by Friday this week) FIXED/ HIGH RETURN ON EFFORT	Job appraisal for Joe (a major management task)
Buy Mary a birthday card (birthday is tomorrow) FIXED/HIGH RETURN ON EFFORT	Financial report for board meeting (vital business information)
Ring Eric re tennis match (this is happening this week) FIXED/ LOW RETURN ON EFFORT	Lunch with the FD of Bide-a Wee (valuable business activity)
E-mail French office about new Bordeaux account (the sooner they know the better) HIGH RETURN ON EFFORT	Ring Personnel about advert for new secretary (pressing need for new secretary)
Ring Personnel about advert for new secretary (Urgent need for new secretary) HIGH RETURN ON EFFORT	9.30 meeting with Frank about office reorganization in September (important business activity)
Talk to Nigel about lateness and poor performance (this must be corrected fast) HIGH RETURN ON EFFORT	E-mail French office about Bordeaux account (high possibility of profitability)

IMMINENCE	*IMPORTANCE*
Job appraisal for Joe (he is probably expecting this soon) HIGH RETURN ON EFFORT	Check up on deliveries to JR Brown (important business information)
Financial report for board meeting (board meeting is next month and this is a long job) FIXED/HIGH RETURN ON EFFORT	Canteen pricing memo (timely information to staff)
Canteen memo to staff (they need to know fairly soon) LOW RETURN ON EFFORT	Business mileage for sales reps (routine task)
Business mileage LOW RETURN ON EFFORT	Old memos to Beryl (routine info)
Cats to the vet (can be done within the next few weeks – not urgent) LOW RETURN ON EFFORT	Cats to the vet (not a business task)
Old memos to Beryl (not urgent) LOW RETURN ON EFFORT	Ring Eric re tennis (not a business task)
Throw out old magazines (You've had them since the 1960s! They can wait for another few years) LOW RETURN ON EFFORT	Throw out old magazines (unimportant – unless of course space is suddenly at a real premium)

So a possible schedule for these tasks might look like this:

9.00   Fill in passport forms and send to Passport Office
9.15   E-mail French office re new Bordeaux account
9.30   Meeting with Frank re office reorganization
10.30   Prepare report for group meeting
11.30   Ring personnel re ad for new secretary
12.00   Make appointment with Nigel for 4.00 this afternoon re performance issues
12.10   Draft canteen pricing memo and send out
12.25   Leave for lunch with FD of Bide-a-Wee
12.30   Lunch
2.00   Buy card for Mary on way back to office
2.15   Delegate deliveries check for JR Brown and sales reps mileage to secretary
2.45   Group meeting
3.45   Prepare for meeting with Nigel
4.00   Meeting with Nigel
5.00   Start draft of financial report for Board meeting
6.00   Ring Eric re tennis on Friday

Outstanding
Beryl's old memos
1960s magazines!

Filing

Customer invoices – options for organizing:
The actual invoices:

Alphabetically by customer, then chronologically by invoice date and if necessary then numerically by invoice number (if there are a number of invoices for different items received on the same day).
Invoice information (ledger or computerized database):

All the above information, but also within the system it should be possible to see when the invoices were paid and the time it took to pay the invoice (for chasing up debtors). It should also be possible to sort the invoices by items invoiced (bananas, grapefruit, lemons, oranges).

It is also useful to have a running total of invoice values.

Sales calls:

Geographical area (if applicable) then alphabetically by customers, then chronologically by date and time of calls.
Apart from the basic customer details (company name, address, telephone/fax/e-mail addresses, contact name etc.) each entry should also contain details of the outcome (orders taken, problems, etc.) of each call and any actions that might need to be taken and any new or altered customer information that was discovered during the call.
It might also be useful to keep a time log of all calls made.

When organizing business information you need to ask these questions:

Who/what is this record about?
When did/will this happen?
What information do I need to record? How will I delete out of date information?
What pieces of information do I need to make comparisons between?
What statistics do I need to produce from this information?
How can I output this information so it is easily understandable?

Chapter 11 Working in teams

Group norms discussion

Perhaps dress codes, use of names, punctuality (or lack of it), jargon/slang/special phrases, attitudes to management or control, openness, formality or informality, attitudes to sharing.

A new team

- Why was I seconded into the team? What is my role here? What tasks will I be expected to complete?
- What are the team's objectives? How will these be measured?
- What are the time scales involved?
- Where will we be working?
- Whom do I report to?
- What budget is involved?
- Who is the customer? What do they need? If we don't know, how are we going to find out?
- Who can help me?

- Who can I go to for help?
- If the leader is absent, who looks after the team?
- How should my results be communicated?

Additional Reading

John Adair
Effective Time Management: How to save time and spend it wisely
Pan Books, London, 1988

Steven Beebe and John T. Masterson
Communicating in Small Groups: Principles and practices
Harper Collins, USA, 1989

Derek Biddle and Robin Evenden
Human Aspects of Management
Institute of Personnel Management, London, 1989

John Crawley
Constructive Conflict Management: Managing to make a difference
Nicholas Brealey Publishing Limited, London, 1992

Richard I. Daft
Management
The Dryden Press, USA, 1988

Arthur D. Jensen and Joseph C. Chilburg
Small Group Communication: Theory and application
Wadsworth Publishing Company, USA, 1991

Gavin Kennedy, John Benson and John McMillan
Managing Negotiations: How to get a better deal
Hutchinson Business, 1989

Dorothy Leeds
Powerspeak: The complete guide to public speaking and presentation
Judy Piatkus (Publishers) Ltd, London, 1988

Index